LEABHARLANNA CHONTAE NA GAILLIMHE
(GALWAY COUNTY LIBRARIES)

GT

Acc. No. D174,477   Class No. 324.24

Date of Return	Date of Return	Date of Return

Books are on loan for 21 days from date of issue.

Fines for overdue books: 10c for each week or portion of a week plus cost of postage incurred in recovery.

Acknowledgements

Margaret, my partner, my daughter Caroline, Kathy Gallagher, John Roche Wexford, Barbara Duffy, Seán Sherwin (Fianna Fáil HQ), Seán McCormack (Berry Print Group), Michael McLoughlin (Berry Print Group), Louise, Shane and Gráinne (Berry's Stationery Shop)

174, 477
€15.00

Previous publications by Manco Publications
The History of Kerry's Winning All-Irelands by Donal Ó'Shea (1987)
Tralee – Street by Street by Donal Ó'Shea (1988)

Printed by Berry Print Group, Westport, Co. Mayo.

Published by:
Manlo Publications, Cloonkeen, Castlebar, Co. Mayo.
Tel.: 087 9004128
mardo@eircom.net

Dedication

To my dear grandchildren Finn, Orla, Eoin, Aishling and Martha.

and Conor

The founding father

Contents

Foreword 7
Events Leading up to the Formation of the Party 9
End of the Civil War and Reorganising of Sinn Féin 14
First Ard Fheis 24
Entering the Dáil 28
Fianna Fáil Comes to Power 31
The Economic War 34
The Constitution 40
Anglo-Irish Agreement 42
The War and Neutrality 45
Seán Lemass 49
Lemass becomes Taoiseach 67
Jack Lynch 71
Lynch reaches the top 73
Troubles in the North 75
The Arms Trial 83
Jack Lynch - Part Two 88
Charles J. Haughey – The Early Years 98
Haughey – His first Ministry is Justice 101
Haughey in Agriculture 105
Haughey is now Number Two 108
Haughey's First Term as Taoiseach 110
Haughey Back as Taoiseach after Eight Months 117
Haughey in Charge in Opposition 121
Haughey and the Great Economic Recovery 125
The Beginning of the End for Haughey 128
The Challenge for the Leadership 131
Albert Reynolds – The Taoiseach from Longford 136
Reynolds Ventures into Petfoods 139
The Longford News 140
Coalition of Fianna Fáil Collapse 141
The Ins and Outs of the Fianna Fáil – Labour Coalition 144
Spring Pulls the Rug on Coalition 148
Ahern the Reuniter of the Party 152
Ahern finally becomes Taoiseach 155
Ahern's Second Term as Taoiseach 158

For Bibliography

(1) *Éamon De Valera* by the Earl of Longford & Tomas P. O'Neill.

(2) Supplement of the *Irish Times* on the Death of Éamon De Valera.

(3) *The Irish Answer* by Tony Gray.

(4) *The Big Fellow* by Rex Taylor

(6) *Up Dev* by Kevin Boland.

(7) *Seán Lemass* by Michael O'Sullivan.

(8) *Seán Lemass* by Brian Farrel.

(9) *Seán Lemass* by John Horgan.
'50 years of Fianna Fáil' – Supplement in *Irish Press* May 26 1976.

(10) 'An Interview with the Minister for Finance' in the Fianna Fáil university magazine. 9 vol. 1, no. 3, 1968.

(11) '500 were at the first Ard Fheis' – an article in Iris Fianna Fáil by Tommy Mullins, February 1983.

(12) 'Seán Lemass' – an article on Seán Lemass by Vincent Brown in *Nusight*.

(13) *Jack Lynch- – a biography* by T. P. O'Mahoney.

(14) 'The gamesmanship of Honest Jack' – An article on Jack Lynch by Godfrey Barker in Sir James Goldsmith's Magazine *Now*.

(15) 'Down to the last hero' an article on Charley Haughey in *In Dublin* magazine by John Healy, October 1986.

(16) *Nice Fellow* – a biography of Jack Lynch by T. Ryle Dwyer.

(17) *The Short Fellow* – A biography of Charles J. Haughey by T. Ryle Dwyer.
The making of a Taoiseach – article in *Magill*.

(18) *The Power Game* by Stephen Collins.

(19) *Albert Reynolds 'The Longford Leader'* by Tim Ryan.

(20) *Bertie Ahearn – Taoiseach and Peacemaker* by Ken Whelehan and Eugene Masterson.

(21) *Dublin Made Me* by C.S. Andrews.

(21) *Men of no Property* by C.S. Andrews.

(22) *Inside Fianna Fáil* by Dick Walsh.

The Irish Times

Independent Newspapers

The Examiner

RTÉ programmes on "Former Taoishigh"

Foreword

"It's all about class, baby, all about class", was what an avid Fianna Fáiler said to Olivia O'Leary when she asked him what Fianna Fáil meant to him. Yes, I suppose, if you pardon the pun, that is a good definition, as not alone does Fianna Fáil appeal to all classes as a 'catch all party' but it has consistently appealed to about 40% of the electorate of all classes since its inception in 1926, eighty years ago. It has always taken a combination or mish-mash of Fine Gael-led coalitions of differing creed to put Fianna Fáil out of power. When they succeed in doing this, they have never been returned for a second period, and Fianna Fáil

Donal O'Shea

have always been brought back to pick up the pieces. Even when the Fine Gael led Rainbow Coalition was elected in mid-term, on the fall of the Albert Reynolds led Fianna Fáil Government, due to the paedophile priest dilemma, they were not returned in the next election and the reins were again entrusted to Fianna Fáil.

In 1973, after the arms trial, Fine Gael and Labour slapped together a twelve-point plan, one point of which was to give £9.50 directly to every housewife in the country. They failed miserably to carry out this plan and were duly dumped out of office in 1977, following which Fianna Fáil were returned by a majority of twenty seats. Parties like Fine Gael and Labour find it easy to criticise and promise the earth in opposition but put them in power and they always fail to deliver. The Garret Fitzgerald led Fine Gael-Labour Coalition of 1982-87 talked about financial rectitude until the dogs in the street were talking about financial rectitude; yet by the time they left office in 1987 they had doubled the national debt. It looks like they were made for opposition. The main ploy by Fine Gael has always been to attack the integrity of Fianna Fáil personalities. However if one was to take the indiscretions of Fine Gael personal as against the number of deputies they have had in the Dail vis-à-vis the number of Fianna Fáil deputies, their ratio would be far greater.

Fianna Fáil have been mainly responsible for taking the country from a 19th Century backward agrarian society to a 21st Century booming economy, one of the fastest growing economies in Europe, if not the world. This has been brought about by a series of well thought out strategies; first of all, De Valera established an excellent base for advancement when he led Fianna Fáil into power in 1932. He abolished the land annuities and the office of the Governor General. He got the ports back from the British on the brink of the Second World War, thus keeping Ireland out of the war in spite of huge pressure from the USA and the UK. He established a written constitution for the country and got housing and education strategies on stream. Seán Lemass got the industrialisation of the country under way with the First and Second Economic Plan. Donagh O'Malley brought about free education which gave every child a chance of secondary education. The combination of Lemass's introduction of foreign investment, together with a suitably, qualified population was the embryo of the Celtic Tiger of the late 90's and to date. Add in the steady influence of Jack Lynch, the vision of Charlie Haughey, the one-page decisiveness of Albert Reynolds and the industrial relations ability of Bertie Ahern and we now see why we are enjoying the wealth never experienced before, at all levels.

As Seán Lemass always said, "a rising tide lifts all boats". It's no wonder the opposition try to zone in on a few – a very few – areas and try to magnify them into major problems. The good thing for Fianna Fáil is that the country is now educated and will not allow parties like this to go into government and take away the good times with their usual 'hair-shirt' politics. We were also lucky to have had Finance Ministers of the calibre of McSharry, Reynolds, Ahearn, McCreevy and presently, Brian Cowen, who not alone got rid of huge debt but brought us into surpluses. One of the most inspiring saving plans ever thought up was that of Charlie McCreevy – the SSIA scheme. In the period of 1973-1977, during a Liam Cosgrave, Fine Gael/Labour Coalition, Jack Lynch, the then leader of the opposition, became know as the 'Real Taoiseach'.

Today, on its 80th birthday, one could say that Fianna Fáil is the Real Government.

The author with Éamon Ó Cuív TD, Minister for Community, Rural and The Gaeltacht, and Mary Coughlan, Minister for Agriculture.

Events Leading up to the Formation of the Party

On December 6th, 1921, the Plenipotentiaries who had gone to London signed the Treaty, and thus created a division in an Irish Nation that had fought and won the War of Independence between 1919 and 1921.

The group that went to London was comprised of Arthur Griffith, Michael Collins, Robert Barton, Erskine Childers, a secretary and two lawyers, Eamonn Duggan and Charles Gavin Duffy. It was what appeared to be a perfectly blended and balanced delegation and their instructions were very specific. There has been a lot of discussion as to whether the Delegates had the power to sign the Treaty or not so that anybody looking at these instructions to-day will see that the instructions were very clear and stated that the plenipotentiaries were to report back before they signed the treaty.

INSTRUCTIONS TO THE PLENIPOTENTIARIES FROM THE CABINET

1. The Plenipotentiaries have full power as defined in their credentials.
2. It is understood, however that before decisions are finally reached on the main questions that a despatch notifying the intention of making these decisions will be sent to the members of the Cabinet in Dublin and that a reply will be awaited by the Plenipotentiaries before the final decision is made.
3. It is also understood that the complete text of the draft Treaty will be similarly submitted to Dublin and a reply awaited.
4. In the case of a break the text of the final proposals from our side will be similarly submitted.
5. It is understood that the Cabinet in Dublin will be regularly informed on the progress of the negotiations.

The Plenipotentiaries left for London in the second week of October 1921, taking with them a draft of the Treaty. This had been prepared by De Valera, Gavin Duffy and Childers.

This was their guide or 'Bible', as it were, as to what would be accepted. Fundamental to the contents of the draft was the term *'External Association'*. Initially, De Valera had looked at the Truce Negotiations pessimistically and was just hoping to use the time to re-organise the troops, re-equip and have a good rest. On September 7th, however, De Valera received a letter from Lloyd George, requesting him "to call a conference to ascertain how the Association of Ireland with the Commonwealth of Nations, known as the British Empire, can best be reconciled with the Irish National Aspirations". This letter gave De Valera great hopes of a peaceful settlement.

De Valera tried to get this matter discussed at cabinet level and failed. Then one morning, prior to the next cabinet meeting, a 'flash of genius' came to him while tying his bootlaces. The key word was *External*. From this he coined the phrase *'External Association with the British Empire'*. Later that day he discussed this at the cabinet meeting and they unanimously understood what he meant and saw the significance of the phrase in the Irish context.

From the records, it can be seen that the plenipotentiaries clearly breached the cabinet instructions, in particular numbers 2, 3 and 4. While they clearly did not adhere to the instructions of the cabinet, neither did they conform to the most significant clause – in fact the key clause in the Draft Treaty, i.e. *'External Association'* with the British Empire. The Pro-Treatyites afterwards argued that the difference between what they obtained in the Treaty and what De Valera wanted was so small as not to be worth fighting about or fighting for. De Valera's reasoning of it was that if it was so small that the British would not wage the terrible war, that the Pro-Treatyites were claiming that the British were threatening, if they did not sign the treaty. De Valera said, "I was ready to break if we didn't get it, because I felt that the distance between the two was so small that the British would not wage war on account of it . . . but I say that small difference is the difference. The fight has lasted all the centuries and I would be willing to win that little sentimental thing that would satisfy the aspirations of the country."De Valera in trying to find a answer to the impasse, produced a paper ,which became known as Document No. 2.

What really was the 'difference' between the Treaty and Document Number 2? Two key points were that:
1. The clauses governing defence envisaged a definite end to British occupation after five years.
2. The Oath of Allegiance.

De Valera was to prove within the next sixteen years that it was possible for the plenipotentiaries "to have stuck to their guns" for Document Number 2. In 1936, he got rid of the Oath of Allegiance and in 1938 he got back the ports. Getting back the ports from Britain on the brink of a "world war only proves that it could have been achieved in 1922 when Britain did not really need them as urgently."

The Treaty then fell far short of what cabinet had agreed to and accepted earlier. The tragic thing was that the plenipotentiaries had broken these policies and knew it. In fact, Collins stated that he had "signed his death warrant". How had Collins and Griffith allowed themselves to be split from Barton during the London talks? If the Delegation had any misunderstandings of the original documents which they had brought to London, they received a further brief at a Cabinet/Delegation meeting on December 3rd, 1921, which should have jogged their memory. At this meeting, the President, De Valera, took his stand on *'External Association'* with the Crown. He also suggested an amendment to the Oath of Allegiance to make it as easy as possible for the Delegation in their negotiations, and this was as follows:-

I . . . do solemnly swear true faith and allegiance to the Constitution of the Free State, to the Treaty of Association and to recognise the King of Great Britain as head of the Associated States.

At the end of the meeting, the following instructions were agreed to and documented by Colm O'Murchada.

(a) Delegates to carry their original instructions with the same powers.
(b) Delegation to return and say that the Cabinet won't accept the Oath of Allegiance, if not amended, and to face the consequences, assuming that England will declare war.
(c) Decided unanimously that the present Oath of Allegiance could not be subscribed to.
(d) Mr. Griffith to inform Mr. Lloyd George that the Document could not be signed, to state that it is now a matter for the Dáil and try to put blame on Ulster.
(e) On a majority vote it was decided that the Delegation be empowered to meet Sir James Craig if they should think it necessary.
(f) It was decided that the President would not join the Delegation in London at this stage on the negotiations.

Another incident during this meeting which made the Cabinet confident that nothing stupid would happen was when Cathal Brugha told Griffith, "Don't you realise that if you sign this thing, you will split Ireland from top to bottom", and Griffith answered, "I'll not sign the Document, but I'll bring it back and submit it to the Dáil."

When the Delegation was returning to London to conclude their talks, they travelled in two separate parties – one via Dun Laoghaire to Holyhead and the other via Dun Laoghaire to Liverpool. Obviously, there was a split and a section not committed to carry out the proposals as agreed at the Delegation/Cabinet Meeting, or in fact the original proposals. Further evidence of this could be construed by other incidents along the way. For instance, Collins' comment to Tom Cullen on their way to the docks, when he stated, "From Dublin, I don't know whether we are being instructed or confused". When the Delegation met in London, three of them began work on the amendments to the Treaty Documents to comply with the Cabinet instructions. When they had finished this work, Griffith and Collins would have nothing to do with it and refused to put these counter proposals before Downing Street.

It would appear from their actions that Griffith and Collins had their minds made up already to sign the Treaty in its existing form. But why? Why had Collins, who was a brilliant military strategist, allowed Lloyd George to split the Delegation? Surely he was aware of the old British trick, *'Divide and Conquer'*. Why also did he not divulge to the Cabinet on December 3rd that due to Griffith's illness he had taken over as Leader of the Delegation?

From Rex Taylor's biography, *'Michael Collins – The Big Fella'*, one can see from Collins' notes to his London friend, O'Kane, that he was constantly sniping at his Cabinet colleagues back in Dublin. In one of these notes he stated, "to go for a drink is one thing . . . to be driven to it is another". If he and Griffith had played ball with their fellow Delegates and did as they were instructed by the Cabinet in Dublin, and pulled together as a team, they would no doubt have done a better job.

In Tony Grey's book, *'The Irish Answer'*, he suggests the theory that Collins' decision to sign the Treaty was motivated by the Irish Republican Brotherhood – the secret, oath-bound society that De Valera resigned from in 1917 and refused to subscribe to afterwards. In addition, Griffith had given a pledge that Lloyd George held him to on the fatal day that the Treaty was signed. Why should Griffith, who was part of a delegation, give a private pledge without consulting his colleagues? Why did he not mention this pledge at the Delegation/Cabinet meeting on December 3rd?

With the Leader of the Delegation and the previous Leader having their minds made up to sign the Treaty, it was only a matter of time before they would push their colleagues into doing likewise. Lloyd George – the crafty old Welsh Wizard – sensed this and helped Collins and Griffith along the way by threatening "an immediate and terrible war". At the right psychological moment, late on the night of 20th, when Delegates were weary and split, and possibly looking forward to Christmas – a peaceful one at home – he produced two envelopes. He told the Delegates, "Here are two documents. One contains the agreement reached by us today; the other says that the Sinn Féin Representatives refused to come into the Empire. If I send the latter, it means war within three days . . . immediate and terrible war". He tried the same blackmail with De Valera during their July meetings in London. He indicated that De Valera would be blamed for causing the war. De Valera called his bluff, stating that the war would be Lloyd George's responsibility. Nothing happened. Finally, Collins and Griffith got the others to sign the fateful Treaty in the early hours of December 6th, 1921. When the representatives came back from London, a meeting of the Dáil was convened for the 8th December at the Council Chamber of U.C.D.and as T.S. Andrews explains in his book 'Dublin Made Me' signs of the coming acrimony began to appear. De Valera declared that he could not ask the Dáil or the people to ratify the Treaty. A month later the Dáil accepted the Treaty by 64 votes to 57 and a Provisional Government was set up. Dev was stripped of all his power and Arthur Griffith was appointed President. Dev and the 56 others, who rejected the Treaty set up Cumann na Poblacht to fight it. There had been hope that the I.R.A. would remain united and that they would take control of the institutions of State. This was further enhanced, when an army officer's Convention was called by the Minister of Defence and sanctioned by the cabinet. This changed, however, when at a later stage the cabinet, including, Mulcahy, the Defence Minister banned the Convention, stating that anyone attending it would automatically expel themselves from the I.R.A. The Conventions, however, went ahead in March, but the split in the Dáil caused a split in the I.R.A and Rory O'Connor and Liam Lynch refused to accept General Mulcahy as Minister of Defence instead of Cathal Brugha. With the election of the Provisional Government, the withdrawal of the British army and the handing over of the barracks, it became obvious that the army that was being set up in Beggar's Bush, the first to be handed over, was a professional army and that a coup d'etat was being prepared. On the 18th of June O'Connor and the anti-Treaty group took over the Four Courts, the H.Q. of the I.R.A. Ten days later Mulcahy and Collins attacked the Four Courts and thus began the Civil War. De Valera was still trying for peace, but Collins stated that there would be no peace until "The Irregulars" laid down their arms. The Civil War lasted for eight months and in that time we saw the death of Griffith, Collins, Ereskine Childers, Cathal Brugha and 800 others. The death of Liam Lynch in the Knockmealdown mountains, brought it home to the anti-reaty side that they could not win this militarily, which was to lead eventually to the formation of the Fianna Fáil party and entry to the Dáil to fight it politically.

End of the Civil War and Reorganising of Sinn Féin

This is our darkest hour . . . I am confident in the ultimate triumph of our cause. My heart and my desires make almost an agonising appeal to hold on and defy them as long as a rifle and cartridge remain, but my head and my conscience tell me it would not be justifiable. I am afraid we will have to face the inevitable sooner or later, bow to force and resort to other methods . . ."

These words were written in a letter by De Valera to P.J. Ruttledge on the day that Liam Lynch, chief of staff of the I.R.A. was fatally shot in the Knockmealdown mountains in April 1922. Both of these items could be described as some of the important factors which brought the Civil War to an end and heralded the beginning of a new era in Irish history. This could be described as the ending of the military struggle for a united, independent republic and rising it to a higher plane of using "other methods" to achieve that aim. From letters written by De Valera to his Cabinet, P.J. Ruttledge, Mary McSweeney and Austin Stack at the time, it could be seen that De Valera understood that independence by Military Strategy was now lost and that it now required other means – which strategy invariably must mean a political solution.

During the War of Independence against the British, guerrilla tactics were an excellent modus operandi. It was another story using these tactics against the National army of the Free State, the majority of whom only a few short months before were involved in guerrilla tactics themselves against the then common enemy. They now, like the Republicans, knew every trick in the book. De Valera was very much aware of this. In addition, after the Truce and the Treaty, most of the populace had become accustomed to living normally again, and having by now taken sides in the General Election, made it almost impossible for the Republicans to carry on. Again due to the cunning strategy of Lloyd George and the old British strategy of 'divide and conquer', Ireland now found itself with not just two, but with many different points of view. Within the Provisional De Facto Government one had a spread ranging from stepping-stone Republicans to ex-Unionists. In the Republican ranks one had those who still favoured a military solution and those who were now turning towards the idea of carrying on the objective of the Republic by political and Parliamentary means. The former element of the Republicans treated the Free State Legislature as essentially British and entry into it would mean recognition of the British Crown. De Valera and the latter group, while not recognising the legitimacy of the Free State Government, realised that it was accepted in a General Election by the majority of the people and as such, while not in their eyes the de juro Government, was however, by the fact it was there, the de facto Government. The Republicans regarded the Second Dáil as the de juro Government. The Republicans defeated in the 'pact' election just before the Civil War abstained from the Free State parliament, just as they had previously abstained from Westminster. They maintained that the Treaty Delegation had been acting on their behalf and their mandate was a free independent Republic, and to continue The Struggle until that was achieved. They argued that the 'pact' election of 1922 was not a valid election as it had been held under threat of war, and as the Civil War had broken out before the Second Dáil was dissolved, that the Second Dáil was the true Government of the Republic and the Provisional Free State Government only a British puppet.

On April 30th, 1923, Frank Aiken, who had replaced Liam Lynch as Chief of Staff of the Republican army, ordered a ceasefire with the following message – "Soldiers of the Republic, legion of the rearguard, the Republic can no longer be defended by your arms. Further sacrifice of life would now be in vain and continuance of the struggle in arms unwise in the National interest and prejudicial to the future of our cause. Military victory must be allowed to rest for the moment with those who have been allowed to destroy the Republic . . ." The people of Ireland would again rally to the standard, "when they are ready you will be, and your place will be again as of old, with the vanguard."

On May 24th, another order came to "Dump arms . . . other means must be sought to safeguard the Nation's right". From the end of May onward, De Valera concentrated on the reorganisation of Sinn Féin. The Republic army was urged to join Sinn Féin. The road ahead for the Republicans under the umbrella of Sinn Féin was to concentrate on the political scene. The main problem here was that Sinn Féin did not recognise the Free State Legislature and the Oath of Allegiance was a major obstacle. These, together with their pledge of abstention to the electorate was going to make the political policy now being followed a difficult task outside Parliament.

In July 1923, a General Election was called and this was to be the first test of the now reorganised Sinn Féin. At the Sinn Féin Convention in Ennis, De Valera was selected as their unanimous candidate. Even though this was supposed to be a free, democratic election, the Free State Minister of External Affairs, Desmond Fitzgerald, father of the subsequent Fine Gael leader (and Taoiseach) stated, "As long as we are in power, De Valera and every other enemy of our country will have to be on the run". De Valera retorted, "Living or dead, we mean to establish the right of Irish Republicans to work and live for complete liberation of our country . . . if the people of Clare select me . . . nothing but the bullet will stop me". W. T. Cosgrave's Pro-Treaty party fought the election under the title of Cumann na nGaedheal. In spite of the threat of being shot by a Free State policeman and all the other Anti-Republican propaganda that existed, De Valera went to Ennis to campaign, was arrested on the platform and imprisoned at Armour Hill. He was elected by the people of Clare to a Parliament he refused to recognise and had no intention of attending. He defeated the Cumann na nGaedhael candidate by 2 to 1. This was a remarkable result when one considers that only months previously they had gone through what De Valera described as their "darkest hour", the result was even more remarkable when one considers that the newspapers and the Catholic church were vehemently anti-Republican, together with the fact that about 13,000 Republicans and indeed voters were in prison or had emigrated.

A year later De Valera was released from prison. The Republicans still continued to meet in Parliament – the Second Dáil. This principle of the Second Dáil was now creating some snags, because since the creation of the Second Dáil there had taken place two General Elections in which Republicans had not achieved a majority. After the 'pact' election of 1922, the Pro-Treatyites had set up the Provisional Government which Sinn Féin refused to attend or recognise. So where now did the Second Dáil stand legislatively and democratically? Deaths had reduced the number of Republican 'deputies'. In addition, some of the Second Dáil was still in existence. Then there were the Republicans who won seats in the last two elections but did not belong to the Second Dáil. To solve some of these problems a meeting was called for August 7th and 8th, 1924. Attending were all elected Republican deputies and all the Republican survivors of the Second Dáil. De Valera suggested the following solution: "For formal acts on account of continuity . . . it would be wiser to regard the Second Dáil as the de juro Government and legislature, but the whole body of elected members including those just returned should act as a Council of State."

A considerable number of the people who were to be instrumental in founding the Fianna Fáil party, including De Valera himself, were in prison camps in the 1922-1924 period. It was in these very camps that the idea of raising policy to a new plane – a political one – took shape. Meanwhile, on the outside, the Sinn Féin party was building on a policy that was being directed into a blindfolded cul-de-sac of abstention, especially by Mary McSwiney. De Valera was beginning to let his ideas of 'entering the Dáil' filter through, and on August 23rd he wrote to Mary McSwiney, "If the oath were removed, to my mind the question of going in or remaining out would be a matter purely of tactics or expediency". De Valera's craftiness was to change around the question of abstention from being a straight-jacketed principle to mere political policy or tactic. In 1924, De Valera and his cohorts were released in a grand amnesty, but by that time Mary McSwiney, and indeed the Sinn Féin party had strengthened its rigidity on the question of the abstention.

On the other hand, a number of the members who were to be the future prominent people in Fianna Fáil were getting disillusioned by the obsession with abstentionism to the exclusion of everything else.

According to Tommy Mullins, many years later, the people experienced a great depression having lost the war and seen their loved ones take the emigrant ship. By mid 1925, it became clear that Sinn Féin policies were not going to achieve anything. The began to get down to the business of organising meetings and forming cumainn. Seán Lemass, released earlier than the others, was successful in a by-election in Dublin in November 1923. He became Minister of Defence in the republican government, replacing Frank Aiken who was finding it difficult to carry out the Defence Ministry portfolio and be Chief of Staff of the army at the same time. Frank remained on as Chief of Staff. Shortly after this, three of the stronger republicans – Gerry Boland, Seán Russell and 'Pa' Hayes, under the tutelage of Lemass went to Russia to acquire arms to renew the Civil War but came back empty handed. It began to appear to Lemass that another armed revolution was out of the question and that the energies of Sinn Féin should be devoted to political action. Between September 1925 and January 1926, in a series of five articles in *An Phoblacht*, the party organ, Lemass attacked the policies and organisation of Sinn Féin, (of which he was a member of the standing committee). He maintained that they should now concentrate on an immediately recognisable political aim like 'The Abolition of the Oath of Allegiance'. His articles caused a considerable stir in the party and members bitterly attacked him in the columns of that same paper.

P.J. Rutledge, who was editor of *An Phoblacht,* was also showing his misgivings about the organisation and the future of the party. In his book, *Dublin Made Me*, Todd Andrews recalls at about this time also, a conversation in Bewley's Cafe with future Irish Press organiser-in chief, Bob Brennan about the fact that the Sinn Féin organisation was "threshing about aimlessly", hinting that a change in policy was imminent.

Other areas that contributed to the unease in its members was that due to the 'one track mind' abstentionist policy of Sinn Féin, everything else that the elected deputies should be doing, i.e. looking after their constituents, was not taking place, particularly with the social problems of the day, like housing, health and unemployment. De Valera had stated to Austin Forde of the *Irish World* in New York that these same constituents, "Our friends are mostly the poorer section and have suffered most". They no doubt would be the most in need of housing, health benefits and employment. However, the elected deputies for Sinn Féin, in addition to be abstentionist would have little communication with any of the Free State administration and agencies whom they hated, so the chances of achieving any benefits for the constituents would be minimal. The National University at the time was made up mainly of Pro-Treatyites with only Hugh Ryan and Arthur Cleary of the senior staff of republican mould. This however, did not prevent the starting up of the UCD Republican Club, which was mainly made up of Ernie O'Malley, Todd Andrews, Andy Cooney, Tadhg Forbes, Frank Ryan and Phyllis Ryan. It was named the Republican Club (rather than Sinn Féin) so as to attract all republican elements under its umbrella. This would indeed open the thinking within the educational establishment to a wider thinking than just 'Abstentionism'. It was not an exclusive student boy, many of the members being graduates and people of note. Arthur Cleary was Chairman, Conor Maguire, Secretary and Treasurer, and Hannah Sheehy-Skeffington, one of the most active women. The first meeting was held at the house of Countess Plunkett in Elgin Road. As the National University and Trinity College were each allotted three parliamentary seats, their main objective being that in the event of a General Election, they would put forward and support republican candidates. Their activities were mainly raising funds and supporting republican charities by means of dances and whist drives. Their members, of course, had plenty of contact and discourse with Sinn Féin headquarters in Suffolk Street.

In November 1925, the army decided to break away from the Republican Government because of the consideration several people in Sinn Féin were giving to entering the Free State Parliament. In face, when the news broke in December that the boundary agreement had been signed, thus accepting partition once and for all, many Republicans wanted to enter the Dáil to defeat the agreement. A meeting of all Republican Deputies with the leader of the Labour Party was held at the Shelbourne Hotel with a hope that "the meeting will afford of reuniting the people of all parties throughout the country in effective opposition to partitioning our motherland". It was also know that a number of Cumann na nGael deputies were willing to vote against the ratification. If the Sinn Féin Deputies had been with the Labour and dissident Cumann na nGael Deputies in the Dáil they could have defeated the ratification of the boundary agreement. However, the Republicans withstood the request of Labour to enter the Dáil, due to their pre-election pledge. This however was to be the final nail, as it was now found that Sinn Féin was in no position to offer an effective opposition to this matter of the utmost importance and added to their frustrations of being unable to capitalise on the affair.

De Valera was to state to Austin Forde, editor of the *Irish World* in New York that it was now clear "that to remain as we were meant ultimate extinction as an effective political force – reduced to some such position as the French Monarchists". It had been believed that the Commission Report was certain to recommend the transfer over of half the six counties to the Free State, particularly of those areas that were predominantly nationalist. When the Commission Report came out however, there was little of no change in the border, but the whole thing was gift-wrapped in a tripartite agreement which included a write-off of the British National Debt of £160m.

"The ratification of the boundary agreement by the 'Elected Native Government' under contract with the enemy to maintain his overlordship", registered as an international agreement in The Hague, together with Sinn Féin's complete helplessness, was no doubt the key that swung so many of the Sinn Féin members towards a new party. It was no doubt that with this missed opportunity, plus De Valera's fear that in time, Republican's philosophy would weaken and fade away, that he decided at the Sinn Féin Ard Fheis on March 9th, 1926 at the Rotunda to propose, "That once the admission oaths of the twenty-six and six county assemblies are removed, it becomes a question not of principle, but of policy whether or not Republican representatives should attend these assemblies."

However, a counter motion, proposed by Fr. O'Flanagan was carried by a tiny majority – so tiny that De Valera could have opposed it. The question is – did he want to? Had he made up his mind to break and form a new party? This gave him the chance, so he resigned. Lemass was already thinking of a new party as he wanted to break from the 'cranks' in Sinn Féin. It was believed that De Valera wanted to get out of politics and only Lemass's idea of a new organisation appealed to him. There is also a story that Gerald Boland wanted to make the break and went wound the assembled hall of 500, ensuring that those who were contemplating voting against De Valera's proposal did just that, knowing a defeat would drive De Valera to forming a new party. After tendering his resignation, De Valera left the hall and was followed by a substantial number of members, including Lemass. Lemass now was to become the main driver behind the formation of the new party. He quickly formed a committee of people who had supported De Valera's motion. Within weeks of the Ard Fheis, a meeting was held at the Sandymount house of Colonel Maurice Moore. Present were De Valera, Lemass, S.T. O'Kelly, S. MacEntee, Ruttledge, Dr Ryan and Gerald Boland. Here the Fianna Fáil party was founded. Ruttledge was elected Chairman, S.T. O'Kelly

Vice-Chairman, Lemass and Boland Joint Secretaries, MacEntee and Ryan Joint Treasurers, with De Valera refusing to take office. The next major meeting was held in Suffolk Street over the office of Sinn Féin headquarters. This was held on Good Friday, 1926. This meeting was presided over by De Valera, Lemass acting as secretary. Also present were Paddy Brennan, Liam O'Doherty, Hannah Sheehy-Skeffington, Ben Doyle, Dr Patrick McCarville, P.L. Sweeney, Tom Derrig, Gerry Boland and Seán McEntee. At that meeting Liam Pedler was proposed General Secretary, seconded by Paddy Brennan. De Valera's proposal that the name of the new party would be Fianna Fáil was also seconded by Brennan. After the establishment under the Chairmanship of Countess Markieviez to organise the Dublin constituencies, North, South and County, Paddy Brennan was appointed secretary of this committee.

It is somewhat confusing as to whether the party was founded at the meeting in Colonel Moore's house or the meeting in Suffolk Street. The name Fianna Fáil was selected at the meeting in Suffolk Street. The name itself was adapted from a variation of the name Óglaith na hÉireann of the Volunteer of 1913, (often called Fianna Fáil by the Gaelic speakers), and the ancient mythological army of Fionn Mac Cumhaill – The Fianna.

Just prior to these meetings there was a feeling that De Valera would form another party, Clann Éireann, founded by a number of supporters who had broken away from the Free State government over the Boundary Commission result. He quashed this rumour very quickly with an interview on April 14th saying, "We . . . are forming a new organisation . . . We are convinced that . . . the ideal of the majority of the Irish people . . . is the Republican ideal and that the people can be banded together for the pursuit of that ideal . . ."

In an interview to the Press on April 17th, De Valera set out the aims of the new party:

". . . Fianna Fáil has for its purpose the reuniting of the Irish people... for the tenacious pursuit of the following aims, using . . . such means as are rightly available.

(1) Securing the political independence of a United Ireland as a Republic.

(2) The restoration of the Irish Language and the development of a native Irish culture.

(3) The development of a social system in which as far as possible, equal opportunity will be afforded to every Irish citizen to live a noble and useful Christian life.

(4) The distribution of the land of Ireland so as the get the greatest

number possible of Irish families rooted to the soil of Ireland.

(5) *The making of Ireland as an economic unit, as self-contained and self-sufficient as possible, with a proper balance between agriculture and other essential industries.*

The very reason for the party, obviously the first aim was going to be the most difficult to achieve. After the Republic was achieved, the other aims would be the policy of the party. This was emphasised. Undoubtedly in the pledge, which had to be signed by candidates:

> *"I support Fianna Fáil . . . in every action . . . to secure the independence for a united Ireland under a Republican Government . . . I will not take . . . an oath of allegiance to a foreign power and if called upon . . . to resign that office, I shall immediately do so".*

From this one can see that unity was the prime aim of the party. We will see also from his speech at the first public meeting of the new party at the La Scala Theatre on May 16th 1926 that the oath of allegiance was the principle barrier to their aim and had to be removed.

> *"The day of Republicans . . . To secure common action . . . of the nation's advance . . . A young man examining the situation would see . . . The country partitioned . . . An assembly of representatives . . . claiming to rule . . . by the majority of the people . . . yet, he would know that nearly one half of the electorate were shut out . . . and that two thirds were opposed in spirit to the existing regime. He would have no difficulty in tracing the anomaly to the oath of allegiance to a foreign power acquiesced in by the majority under the duress of an external threat of war",* which, *"He would recognise as an immediate obstacle to a unified national effort . . . To any support from . . . abroad and a screen by which England's controlling hand was . . . concealed from . . . the Irish people from the outside world and by isolating the oath . . . England's . . . control would be exposed . . . He could see ahead once the oath was destroyed a further advance . . . cutting the bonds of foreign interference . . . until full internal sovereignty of the twenty-six counties was established . . . Finally . . . the solution . . . of successfully bringing in the North . . ."*

De Valera looking through the eyes of 'a young man's' vision of Fianna Fáil also reiterated the futility of further war and the use of democratic parliamentary means as the only way to achieve the objectives.

"He would realise that a successful uprising . . . of a subject people is . . . impossible, whilst an elected native government under contract with the enemy . . . stands in the way . . . the . . . horrors of a Civil War alone are a sufficient . . . deterrent to prevent . . . such an uprising. He would conclude that the necessary condition . . . was the removal of a Government subservient to a foreign master from De Facto control . . . and the removal of the oath was an essential preliminary".

De Valera also showed his wishes for reconciliation for the benefit of the nation as a whole when he stated in his speech, "Means must be found to bring the national forces together – at least to this extent, that the two sections will be in a common direction so that the resultant of their efforts may be the greatest possible".

De Valera's speech mainly concerned the oath and its abolition. He stated that, "For me, it is enough that it is called and 'oath' officially . . . and whenever it suits it will be held to be an oath by those who impose it and will be so understood by the world". He continued, "Why retain it as an instrument for our national and moral degradation . . . for lying and perjury for the whole world?"

These are extracts from what was the major speech at La Scala even though De Valera proclaimed he was not there in any official capacity but as "A private and with a private's liberty".

The National movement had once again begun and nobody was left in any doubt what the objective was as they all set out for their own constituencies to 'pass on the torch' to a new generation. Funds started to trickle their way into the coffers of the new party from the U.S.A., beginning with £50.00 from the Benjamin Franklin Council of Cleveland. This eventually turned into a flow with a huge contribution from the Association for an Irish Republic in Chicago. A full-scale organisation of the party ensued. All the rules and regulations were drafted in paper. An organising committee was set up under Seán Lemass, and Gerry Boland was chief organiser on the ground. Setting up the organisation on paper wasn't too difficult as they already had the experience and know-how having already done so with the Sinn Féin organisation. Getting it together at ground level proved a lot more difficult. As a lot of bad roads throughout the twenty-six counties had to be travelled in bad cars and coming into the winter, in bad weather. The first step was selecting a key republican in each area. It was easy to pick one out, but it was another job trying to convince them to get involved in this new political party. A lot of them were just getting back to a settled life with their families, some of them were still active in the IRA or 'on the run', some had emigrated and above all, the majority were soldiers, not politicians. It took a lot of burning the 'midnight oil' to convince them that this was the new 'vanguard'. Once a reliable leader was found in each area, he would then be given the task of selecting other key men in the area and building up the Cumainn backed up by representatives sent from headquarters to help develop the formation of the local constituencies. They would then meet on a regular basis.

De Valera at the same time was recognising the key difficulties – the republicans who were being reluctant to go along with the new party and the call to deputies who now accepted his policy to resign their seats.

On June 29th, De Valera decided to visit his Clare constituency. There he gave one of his 'From the Heart' speeches:

"I stand for the Republic, for the full freedom of Ireland as thoroughly today as I stood nine years ago, when I first came to you".

He tried to get the point across that first of all, the existing situation had to be understood so that the problem could be solved and progress made:

". . . for the moment, we have been driven out of the citadel and I am asking for people to attack it again and retake it . . . and I say we can win back the whole of the country for the Republic if we set about it in the right way and do not hamper ourselves with artificial restrictions".

He reminded them of Clare's part in winning Catholic Emancipation in 1829, and that "the oath of allegiance was a denial of their national faith and they should start out now and smash it. He pointed out that he had no intention of resigning his seat and for those Sinn Feiners who tried to tie him down to a specific future policy he retorted:

"to pledge ourselves . . . to every step we shall take and the moment we shall take it would be absurd . . . factors determining the tactics of the situation cannot be gauged until the exact moment has arrived and all . . . circumstances fully known".

First Ard Fheis

On a mild, sunny Wednesday, November 24th 1926, on the fourth anniversary of the execution of Erskine Childers, and the city alive with the noise of barges, trams, horses and fruit sellers, the Fianna Fáil Party launched its first Ard Fheis. The venue was the Rotunda building in Parnell Square where 500 delegates, mostly over thirty, with a sprinkling of women and priests arrived from all over the thirty-two counties.

A directive was given from the Ard Fheis to the National Executive to co-operate with all Republicans to create a unified front with all anti-imperialists in the six counties, as far as was practical.

Seán T. O'Ceallaigh, T.D., presiding, welcomed the delegates stating that the aim of Fianna Fáil was to unite all those who stood for an Irish Ireland as against those who stood for an English Ireland.

A comprehensive social and economic programme was set out in the CORU (constitution), which was adopted. Six of the first committee of fifteen were women, and one of the committee was the Very Reverend Eugene Canon Coyle from Fermanagh, to make the committee truly representative of the thirty-two counties.

There was some disagreement regarding the name of the party as De Valera wanted Fianna Fáil and Lemass wanted 'The Republican Party'. A compromise was arrived at with Fianna Fáil the main name and 'The Republican Party' as a subtitle.

De Valera, on taking his place on the podium got a wonderfully warm reception. He commented on the deeply-felt affection of the delegates and their unshakeable confidence in his ability to lead the Irish People to freedom. He pointed out the danger of Civil War if constitutional politics were ruled out – the same warning he had given in 1922.

"It is in vain to think that the natural aspirations of Irishmen for the liberty of their country are going to be stifled now. If the road of peaceful progress and natural evolution be barred, then the road of revolution will beckon and will be taken. Positive law and natural right will be again bloodily fought out, and when the fight is over it will probably be found out once more that the problem has remained and that force is not the solution".

De Valera was unanimously elected President. Seán Lemass and

Gerald Boland were elected joint Secretaries on a full-time basis, and their tremendous work over the next five years throughout the country was responsible for the rapid establishment of one of the most powerful political organisations ever known. The full list of Officers elected was a follows: -

President: De Valera
Vice-Presidents: Seán T. O'Kelly and P.J. Ruttledge
Honorary Secretaries: Seán Lemass and Gerald Boland
Honorary Treasurers: Dr. J. Ryan and Seán MacEntee
National Executive: Frank Aiken, T. D., T. Deirg,
Rev. E Coyle P.P., M. Kilroy, T.D., Dan Breen, Mrs. M. Pearse,
Madame Markievcz, P.J. Little, Mrs. Tom Clarke,
Dr. Con Murphy, Prof. E. Mullen, Prof. P. Caffrey,
Dorothy McArdle, Mrs. Sheehy-Skeffington, Miss L. Kearns.

In the early months of 1927, preparations were being put in place for the forthcoming General Election. De Valera had to take some time off to appear as a witness in a court case in New York. He was there to ensure that monies collected there in 1919 and 1920 for the Government of the Republic of Ireland be returned to the original subscribers and not given to the Free State Government, as they had requested. It was a victory for De Valera. He took advantage of the trip to tour the States drumming up support for the Republican cause and finished up with a very successful rally in Boston. The ship on which he sailed was the *SS Republic*.

When De Valera arrived back, he was straight into an election campaign. Fianna Fáil's policy for the election was principally the abolition of the Oath of Allegiance; the withholding of tax annuities and the imposition of protective tariffs. W. T. Cosgrave and his Cumann na nGaedhal party, far from using the 'stepping stone' argument – used to win the election in 1922 – were advocating honouring the Treaty Agreement – "The sanctity of International Agreements". This reiterated De Valera's previous view that Cosgrave had painted himself into a corner.

The election proved to be an enormous success for Fianna Fáil – a Party formed only thirteen months previously. Fianna Fáil won 44 seats against 47 for Cumann na nGaedhal, (63 in 1922), 22 for Labour, 14 Independents, 11 Farmers, 8 National League and Sinn Féin were reduced from 25 in 1922 to 5. Fianna Fáil had polled over 35% of the vote. After the election, De Valera stated that "Republicans recognise no opponents save the Imperialist (Cumann na nGaedhal) Party".

The next step for Fianna Fáil was to find a way of taking their seats in the Dáil chamber without taking the oath. The procedure for taking the oath was not clear. In 1922, it was done formally in the Chamber by the Speaker. However, in 1923, when it was thought that there might be a Republican demonstration in the Dáil, the procedure was changed whereby now the ceremony was to be carried out by the Dáil Clerk in his room before Deputies were allowed to enter the Chamber. Fianna Fáil sought advice from Counsel, and Counsel's opinion was that neither under the Constitution or the Treaty could a Deputy, (oath or no oath) be excluded from any part of the House before the House was duly constituted, and if so, any Ceann Chomhairle elected in the absence of such deputies, would not be validly elected. This opinion however, was not accepted by the Clerk, Colm Ó Murchada, from the Fianna Fáil Deputies when they attempted to enter the Chamber. De Valera and his Deputies then withdrew and returned to Fianna Fáil headquarters to review the situation.

On July 10th, Kevin O'Higgins, Minister for Home Affairs, was shot dead by an offshoot of the IRA. This prompted the Free State Government to introduce the following:-

[1] The Public Safety Act
This gave "extensive coercive powers against any organisation engaged in treasonable or seditious activities".

[2] The Electoral Amendment Bill
This made it obligatory for a candidate to sign an Affidavit that on being elected he would take the oath or forfeit his seat.

[3] A Bill to abolish the right by which people could initiate by a Petition or a Referendum on a Constitutional Amendment.

These left De Valera and Fianna Fáil with a major dilemma which cut off any opportunity of Constitutional action save by taking the oath and entering the Dáil. Some members of the Party were by now ready to do that and two members, Dan Breen (who had resigned from the Party), and Patrick Belton (who had the Party Whip removed) had already done so.

De Valera, in a letter to one of his American friends, Frank P. Walsh, stated, " (the) way of removing the Oath from the outside is being made impossible".

At a meeting of the National Executive of the Party on August 9th, De Valera pointed out that the choice now was giving up political action or entering the Dáil. He said that it was well known that the Oath was not being administered as an oath. It was agreed on a vote – 44 for and 7 against – to test this by presenting themselves at the Dáil. On the following night, the Fianna Fáil Deputies held a meeting. Boland and Lemass, who for some time had regarded the Oath as an 'Empty Formula', spoke strongly in favour of entering the Dáil. The 42 Deputies signed a document subscribing to the 'Empty Formula' theory, part of which is as follows:-

> *"Is it not uncommonly believed that the required Declaration is not an oath, that the signing of it has no binding significance in conscience or in law. . . . without including this nation in obligations of loyalty to the English Crown . . .*
>
> *They (the Deputies) intend . . . to present themselves at the Clerk's Office of the Free State Dáil for the purpose of complying with the Provisions of Article 17 of the Constitution by inscribing their names in the Book . . . among other signatures appended to the required Formula.*
>
> *. . . The Fianna Fáil hereby give Public Notice that they propose to regard the Declaration as an empty formality and . . . their only allegiance is to the Irish Nation, and that will be given to no other power and authority.*

The author with Mary O'Rourke, the then Minister for Education and Cllr. Frank Chambers, former Senator and Chairman of Mayo County Council.

Entering the Dáil

The very next day De Valera led his Deputies, in threes, into the Clerk's room. He made it quite clear he was not taking an oath but signing the book to comply with the Clerk's request. To emphasise that he was not taking the oath, he removed the Bible from the desk and placed it on a seat at the other side of the room. He then proceeded to cover the top of the book where he believed there may have been some semblance of an oath. He did not even read this statement but signed the book, "The way you would sign an autograph". At the same time he was stating, "I am not prepared to take the oath. I am not going to take an oath. I am prepared to put my name down in this book in order to get into the Dáil, but it has no other significance". The two Deputies accompanying De Valera were Dr. James Ryan and Frank Aiken, who signed the book and followed De Valera into the Chamber, as did the 39 others.

Though this was a major turning point in constitutional politics, as well as the end as such, of abstentionism, history was to prove very quickly that De Valera and his fellow Deputies had taken the right decision. This was to be borne out in the following elections of 1927 and 1932, when Fianna Fáil came to power. Further evidence was the practical extinction of Sinn Féin, whose claim to represent Republicanism disappeared at the ballot box. One might ask why De Valera had not taken the oath in 1922. The issue in question in 1922 was the acceptance of the Treaty. The issues in question in 1927 were primarily the abolition of the Oath, the withholding of tax annuities, and the imposition of protective tariffs. The electorate had endorsed these policies and given Sinn Féin their answer. It was also believed that if Fianna Fáil had not insisted in abstentionism in the first election, they might even have got a majority, as some of the electorate voted for the other, smaller parties on that basis. This was also born out in later elections. Professor Desmond Williams maintains that this was "A great turning point in the history of Parliamentary Government in Ireland".

Fianna Fáil entered the Dáil for the first time on August 12, 1927, and though the opposite sides of the Civil War were facing each other for the first time, and the whole Chamber was very tense, yet the whole session went on very gentlemanly.

On August 16th, the Labour Leader, Thomas Johnson, moved a motion of No Confidence in the Government. Though the combined votes of Fianna Fáil and the smaller parties could bring down the Government, the absence of the National League Deputy, John Jinks of Sligo, from the Chamber meant that the vote was tied. The Speaker of the

House cast his vote in favour of the Government and saved the day for Cumman na nGaedhal.

Due to this close shave, shortly afterwards President Cosgrave called an election for September 15th, [Fianna Fáil increased their position by winning 13 extra seats, up to 57. It increased its share of the vote from 26.1% to 43.9%. The Government however, increased their position by 15 seats, (27% to 30.4%). The smaller parties suffered major losses].

De Valera put forward his policies for Fianna Fáil. Some were reassurances against Cumman na nGaedhal's propaganda "that Fianna Fáil would be revolutionary and attempt too much too quickly". De Valera stated:-

(1)   "Our purpose is not to destroy, but to broaden and widen the Free State assembly, so as to free it from all foreign control and interference, and make it truly representative of the whole people..."

(2)   There would be no dismissals of Civil Servants appointed by the previous Government as "those who took service in the Free State did it believing they were right".

Many prominent clergy spoke against Fianna Fáil from platforms, altars and in letter form. These included Monsignors, Deans and Parish Priests.

Fianna Fáil speeches were kept mostly to economic affairs, particularly their abhorrence of land annuities. These annuities were payments to the British Government as a result of Land Acts in the late 1870's whereby farmers were given loans by the British Government to buy out their farms. They amounted to about £5 million per annum.

The result of the election of September 15th saw Fianna Fáil increase its number of seat by 13 to 57. Cumann na nGaedhal increased their position by 15 seats to 62. The National League lost 6 seats, Labour lost 9, and Sinn Féin found itself unable to field any candidates, further evidence that not only were Fianna Fáil endorsed as the Republican voice, but also it was proof that their entering the Free State Dáil on an 'empty formula' oath was accepted by an overwhelming majority of Republicans. Sinn Féin had been wiped out by Fianna Fáil as effectively as it had done to the Irish Parliamentary Party in 1918. It is important to note as well that Fianna Fáil's successes had been in spite of a most hostile press and media.

So De Valera and Fianna Fáil were now a pretty strong opposition to the Government and this enabled them to build and consolidate over the next five years. This newfound political respectability brought about some acceptability with the Church, particularly helped by his objection to Protestants being appointed to Public Posts, proposing that the Dáil should not meet on Holy Days, and that prayers should be said before each session of the Dáil. By appropriate speeches in the Dáil, he maintained a friendly relationship with the IRA and the Labour Party.

In view of the fact that the national press had given Fianna Fáil a rough ride over the years, De Valera decided to start his own newspaper with American funds. He launched *The Irish Press* in 1931 to support the Party. He was now able to launch bitter attacks on the Government with regard to their incompetence in handling the Boundary commission in 1925, its lack of economic policies which saw no social services, no protection for home industries and agriculture, and lack of public safety measures against the IRA. To get the farmers on his side, he attacked the land annuities as well as keeping Protestants happy by agreeing with other parties to support Douglas Hyde for President. He also strongly proposed the abolition of the Oath of Allegiance.

Fianna Fáil Comes to Power

Approaching the General Election of 1932, Cumman na nGaedhal bitterly attacked Fianna Fáil of being in cohorts with the IRA extremists, who it is said had Communist leanings, on the grounds that De Valera had strenuously opposed the draconian Constitution (Amendment No. 17) Bill. The Government had introduced the Bill in October 1931 in answer to an increase of IRA activities and murders. This Bill was the most drastic Bill ever introduced. It included a military tribunal with powers that included the death penalty, the power to declare associations unlawful and new, wide-ranging powers given to the police. Its election literature maintained that De Valera, "caused one Civil War and was about to create another", and that his election to office would endanger the lives of citizens and the rights of farmers.

J.H. Thomas, Secretary of State for Dominion Affairs, warned the British Cabinet that if De Valera was elected President, a difficult situation would ensue.

Fianna Fáil fought the election on the promise of removing the oath, of withholding the land annuities and that it would not exceed its mandate. It denied Cumman na nGaedhal's accusations of leanings

De Valera with members of the first Fianna Fáil cabinet, 1932.

towards communism, the intention of a new land tax and refusal to pay interest in national loan and bank deposits.

Members of the Free State Government approached the Commander of the Free State troops to find out what he would do if De Valera and Fianna Fáil attained power in the election and he retorted that he would accept De Valera if that was the people's choice.

Fianna Fáil was returned with seventy-two seats against Cumman na nGaedhal's fifty-seven. They were now the largest party in the Dáil and with the support of the Labour Party (reduced to seven seats), formed the Government, with De Valera as President. He also got the support of three Independents, (including James Dillon, future leader of Fine Gael). De Valera also assumed the portfolio of Foreign Affairs.

The new Dáil assembled on March 9th. It was thought amongst Fianna Fáil that Cumman na nGaedhal would not hand over power easily and many Fianna Fáil Deputies entered the Chamber carrying guns, albeit, according to Seán McEntee, without bullets. One Deputy was alleged to have been seen assembling a machine gun in a telephone box in the House. De Valera himself was apprehensive and in fear of assassination. He did not carry a weapon himself, but was accompanied by his son, Vivian, who did.

Contrary to all expectations, the handing over was all done smoothly. Seán Lemass, at the age of 33, became the Minister for Industry and Commerce – the youngest Minister in Europe – a portfolio he was to hold both in Government and in Shadow Cabinet for twenty-seven years until he became Taoiseach. Seán T. O'Kelly became Vice-President and Minister for Local Government; Dr. Jim Ryan, Agriculture; Frank Aiken, Defence; Seán McEntee, Finance; Tom Derig, Education, and P.J. Rutledge in Lands.

Despite Seán Lemass' comment in the Dáil in 1928, that the Party was "slightly constitutional", the Government set out now in a proper constitutional manner to put its mandated policies into action. With immediate acceptance by the army and Civil Service, Fianna Fáil started right away to carry out its programme. As Ireland, and indeed the world, were heading into the Great Depression of the Thirties, his first major decision in Government was to cut salaries of members, including his own salary as President from £2,500 (previous President's) to £1,700. He then set about carrying out the policies which he had put before the electorate, i.e. the removal of the Oath of Allegiance and retention of the Annuities. Mr. J.H. Thomas, Secretary of State for Dominion Affairs tried to imply that the Oath was part of the Treaty and the Annuities were honour bound, by means of special agreements signed by W.T. Cosgrave in 1923 and 1926, though not ratified by the Dáil. Thomas further tried to link both issues.

De Valera on the other hand, decided to keep them separate and first set about the abolition of the Oath by means of a Bill passed by the Dáil on May 18th, 1932 in spite of strong opposition from Cumann na nGaedhal. De Valera at all stages emphasised that the Oath was not compulsory under the Treaty and was a domestic issue to be decided by a domestic legislature.

The Economic War

Once the Bill of removing the Oath had passed through the Dáil, De Valera now decided to turn his attention to the annuities and other payments being made to Britain – meetings of both parties followed in Dublin and London. The British were still trying to discuss both the oath and the annuities. De Valera let them know in no uncertain manner that the Oath would be removed, but agreed that the question of the annuities could be sorted out by arbitration, insisting that the tribunal should not be limited to members of the British commonwealth and that all payments (the annuities were only part) should be discussed.

While the Government were negotiating the personnel for the Tribunal however, a resolution was passed in the House of Commons to impose duties or tariffs on imports of goods from Ireland – to recoup, as it were, the annuity money due from Ireland. The British insisted that this had nothing to do with the abolition of the Oath.

Though the British Government found out that De Valera had deposited the annuity money in a suspense account pending the outcome of the Tribunal, this did not prevent the tariff resolution being passed, thus confirming to De Valera that the financial considerations under discussion were only secondary to the constitutional issues.

On learning this, Lemass, one of the delegates on his way to Ottawa for the Tribunal, contacted De Valera immediately, suggesting counter-measures on Irish imports from Britain – especially coal.

Further meetings in London, by the Leader of the Labour Party, William Norton and later by De Valera himself, failed to prevent Britain imposing tariffs.

In a way, this fell into De Valera's barrow, as part of the government's manifesto was a policy of protection. As the Irish Government were always wary of retaliation, they had not moved on this policy. As Britain had now started the Economic Way, it was much easier for De Valera to embark on the road of a self-sufficient policy and by putting the blame on Britain, would avoid the negative public opinion he would have encountered at home. To further explain his decision to the people, he called out a series of public meetings. He appealed to the farming community to change to tillage; asking the Irish people to buy Irish, thus negating the necessity to import and countering the perceived fall in exports. He pointed out to the people that though as brothers they would suffer in the short-term, things would work out better in the long-term. This policy did indeed work but in the long term, especially with

Lemass succeeding in having industries established behind the protective wall. In fact, industrial employment rose by 43,000 (from 110,000 to 154,000) between 1931 and 1936, which prompted the well-known British economist, John M. Keynes to say in a lecture in UCD in 1933:

> *"If I were an Irishman, I should find much to attract me in the economic outlook of your present Government towards greater self-sufficiency".*

A further meeting by De Valera in London failed to resolve the financial question and further hardened De Valera's thinking that the British stand was more constitutional than fiscal.

In the summer of 1933, another constitutional issue began to surface. The Governor General, Mr. James McNeill – another symbol of monarchical authority – was seen by Irish Republicans to be repulsive to the Irish people. De Valera had hoped that McNeill would stay low-key. When McNeill however, arrived at a French Legation dance, the Government Ministers present walked out. Following a protest by the Governor General it was agreed that the Government would be advised henceforth of the Governor General's social diary, so that similar embarrassments would not occur.

However, a similar situation arose at the Eucharistic Congress, whereby the President received the principal guests, keeping the King's representative in the background. Public protestations by McNeill drew the question of his office and his relationship with the Irish executive into question. This eventually led to McNeill being removed from office by the King. De Valera appointed a Maynooth shopkeeper, Domhnall Ó Buachalla in his place. Ó Buachalla was a former anti-Treaty Deputy and he came to live in an ordinary house in a Dublin suburb, and not in the Vice-Regal Lodge. He kept a low profile.

In September 1932, De Valera presided over the Council of the League of Nations in Geneva and made a major international impression by his rebuke of the larger states and his plea for the plight of small nations, the unemployed, the starving in the world and the rights of people and their families. He stated:

> *"It is our duty to face this anomalous and desperate position frankly and honestly; not as the representatives of states or parties of special interests, but as men who recognise that the primary duty of statesmen, national or international, is to plan for the well-being of their fellows, the plain ordinary human beings of every country".*

The Government was now beginning to come under a storm of criticism from the opposition. De Valera was becoming anxious as well about the 'rattling of swords' being made by a growing army of comrade's association, an organisation of retired officers under the head of Dr. Thomas P. O'Higgins. In one of O'Higgins' speeches, he stated: "We are an army of peace. Policy, however, may not be able to control circumstance".

So in January 1933, De Valera decided that the best way of showing his strength against the British and the Irish opposition was to go to the country. He put forward his policies, which were more or less the same as the previous year; the development of industry by protective tariffs, increased tillage, the retention of the annuities (where now payments from farmers were to be halved), the completion of the abolition of the Oath, (still held up by the Senate), and the abolition of the Senate in its present form. He also voiced his opinion against the proportional representation system of electing Deputies.

Cosgrave's only policy was to end the economic war in three days.

This time Fianna Fáil received an overall majority of 77 seats against 48 for Cosgrave and 28 for others. This was an overwhelming endorsement of De Valera's policies as Fianna Fáil gained 692,000 votes (over 50% of the electorate).

On April 23rd, 1933, De Valera put forward in a speech his *modus operandi* for achieving an independent Republic:

> *"Let us remove these forms one by one so that the State we control may be a Republic, and that when the time comes the proclaiming of the Republic may involve no more than a ceremony".*

He finally got rid of the Oath of Allegiance in May 1933, and in November he had, by means of three amendments to the Constitution, transferred from the Governor General to the Executive Council the function of recommending money Bills plus the power of withholding assent to Bills of all kinds, together with the removal of the right to appeal from Irish courts to the Privy Council in London.

He had already succeeded in down-grading of the office of the Governor General, getting McNeill removed and replacing him with an old friend, Kildare shopkeeper Domhnall Ó Buachalla.

Due to the various amendments to the Constitution by De Valera and Cosgrave since 1922, the Constitution was becoming unruly. This gave De Valera the opportunity to start thinking of a new Constitution which would come from the Irish people themselves, and to satisfy Republican thinking of constitutional continuity from the second Dáil.

De Valera's idea was to fashion a Constitution that would eliminate the function of the King completely from the domestic affairs of the State, but using the King for diplomatic purposes in external affairs, similar to his idea of "external association" that he had first proposed in 1921.

While working on these Constitutional issues, De Valera had some domestic issues that were causing concern. This came in the form of the Blueshirts and the IRA. The Blueshirts evolved from the friendly association of ex-officers headed by Dr. T.F. O'Higgins. The Cumman na nGaedhal party joined up with the centre party and became the United Friendly Party who supported the Blueshirt Movement. Eoin O'Duffy, who had been Chief of Police in Cosgrave's Free State Government, was fired by De Valera when he came to power and took over from O'Higgins and became head of the Blueshirt Movement. The movement had connotations of Hitler's and Mussolini's fascist movements in Europe, and bore its name from the blue shirt uniforms and berets they wore. It was De Valera's belief that their aim was the same as their counterparts in Europe, to overthrow the Government and set up a military dictatorship. Cosgrave himself was Vice-President of the movement and parliamentary leader of the party.

At the same time, the IRA were getting more and more impatient with De Valera's constitutional approach to a united Ireland, and since De Valera had removed the military tribunal, the IRA had begun to parade openly again and were becoming an embarrassment to him. De Valera asked them to hand in their arms and refrain from drilling. They refused unless De Valera promised to declare a Republic within 5 years.

So to put an end to two illegal armies running about the country, De Valera reintroduced the amendment to the Constitution which allowed him to set up military tribunals. He passed legislation banning the wearing of uniforms, the carrying of weapons and, after the IRA had been involved in three brutal murders in a short period of time, he declared them an illegal organisation and proscribed it in June 1936. Within a year the United Ireland Party began to crumble and the period of the Blueshirts eventually ended with O'Duffy leading a small army to fight in the Spanish Civil War.

Other IRA members had adapted to political means and had been incorporated into Fianna Fáil. Some had joined a special auxiliary group of the police as the Broy Harriers, after the name of their Commissioner.

In 1934, some were offered commissions in the regular army, while older members, who had been involved in the Civil Wars, were awarded army pensions.

Meanwhile, on constitutional matters, J.H. Thomas, Dominions Secretary, informed the House of Commons that the Irish Free State, as a member of the British Commonwealth, was free to order its own affairs. De Valera's response was that he understood from this that Britain had decided *". . . not to treat as a cause of war . . . a decision of the Irish people to sever their connection with the Commonwealth"*.

In the autumn of 1935, Malcolm McDonald replaced Thomas as Dominions Secretary and he set out once and for all to reach an amicable settlement with De Valera. This was followed by numerous meetings between the two in London, as De Valera was on his way or coming back from Geneva, where he was having treatment for failing eyesight.

Simultaneously, on June 8th, 1936, the Irish Commissioner, on instructions from De Valera, delivered a memo to King Edward VIII informing him of the Irish Government's intention, at the autumn session of Parliament, to introduce a Bill for the purpose of setting up *"a new constitution . . . to deal with the internal affairs of Saorstát Éireann . . . leaving unaffected the constitutional usages relating to external affairs"*, along with, *"the creation of the Office of President . . . and the abolition of the Office of Governor General"*.

On June 9th, a commission was set up to examine the question of the Senate, which had been abolished by the Fianna Fáil Government.

Meanwhile, in line with McDonald's thinking, there seemed to be a favourable attitude in the British Cabinet for a settlement, even though the Northern Ireland question was a stumbling block. Other issues of note were constitutional, defence, trade, and financial. The British, though they seemingly wanted a settlement, with their usual dithering, began to put conditions on ports (needed for defence), constitutional (must recognise the King), and partition (sidelined). The only issues which seemed open for negotiation were trade and financial. Eventually, De Valera/McDonald talks were getting nowhere and De Valera proceeded to press on ahead with his constitution.

Then, out of the blue in November, came the Abdication crisis of King Edward VIII. On the promptings of Seán McEntee, (England's demise was Ireland's opportunity), De Valera, in two days of guillotine motions in the Dáil, pushed through the External Relations Act, removing the Crown from all domestic functions in the Constitution and leaving the Crown in for diplomatic, external purposes only.

In early 1937, it was acknowledged that the Acts passed by the Dáil in December had not, *"altered fundamentally the position of the Irish Free State as a Dominion"*. They were concerned however, that in De Valera's first draft of the new Constitution, Article I, i.e. *"That the Irish Free State . . . is a co-equal of the Community of Nations forming the British Commonwealth of Nations"*, was being omitted.

De Valera pressed ahead with his Constitution without making any of the amendments the British were suggesting.

The Constitution

Having taken advantage of the abdication crisis to remove the King from the Constitution, De Valera realised that it was necessary to maintain external relationships with the Crown for the purpose of appointing diplomatic and consular representatives, and the conclusion of international agreements, as well as the hope that the link maintained with the Crown would be a step towards the ultimate unification of the country. The statement that the Irish Free State was a co-equal of the British Commonwealth was still a part of the amended constitution. It was not long before De Valera assured Britain that he would not hesitate to repeal the External Relations Act if he could not see it as a vehicle towards reunification. In drafting the new Constitution, the question of the title of the State became a problem. As the new Constitution was not going to cover the whole of the country, it was decided by De Valera that he would use the name of 'Éire'. As the use of another name, Poblacht na hÉireann, (The Republic of Ireland) may at this stage be repulsive to the British Government as well as, the fact that he was envisaging using the term Poblacht na hÉireann when the country was eventually united. In the new draft he deliberately left out the reference that Ireland was a member of the British Commonwealth.

When framing the section of the Constitution dealing with social principles, De Valera wished to ensure that it would not be so rigid as to prevent useful legislation or lead to continuous litigation. Irish thinking at the time was influenced by the events that were happening in Europe With the rise of socialism, fascism and communism, which had the effect of people being more aware of the duties of the State to the people, De Valera had to frame a Constitution, the social principle of which would not run into any major problems.

With this in mind, he sought council from such eminent writers of Catholic theology as Dr. Michael Browne and Dr. Cornelius Lucey of Maynooth College, and Fr. Edward Cahill, a Jesuit, who was also a noted Catholic social writer of the day. Fr. Cahill and Fr. John C. McQuaid supplied various drafts of social thinking based on the Constitutions of Austria, Poland and France, together with various social encyclicals of the different Popes.

De Valera was very concerned that the Constitution he would eventually arrive at would not need great fundamental change when the unity of the country was established, so the next major, and as he later stated, most difficult article of the Constitution was the one dealing with religion. Discussions took place with the Catholic hierarchy and heads of all the various churches in Ireland at the time, and taking Archbishop

Gregg's advice, using the definitions of each Church, as per the records of the Council of Trent, he concluded the article as follows:-

"The State recognises the special position of the Holy Catholic Apostolic and Roman Church as the guardian of the Faith professed by the great majority of the citizens. The State also recognises the Church of Ireland, the Presbyterian Church in Ireland, the Methodist Church in Ireland, the Religious Society of Friends in Ireland, as well as the Jewish Congregations and the other religious denominations existing in Ireland at the date of the coming into operation of this Constitution."

The only objections to the draft in the Dáil were clauses that it was alleged that women should not go outside the home to work, and the powers of the President. Before the Constitution was finally approved by the Dáil on June 14th, 1937, it was decided that the referendum on the constitution was to take place on the same day as the General Election, not alone from the point of view of cost, but it was obvious that a General Election would attract a larger tournout than a plebicite on its own, thus giving the new Constitution the maximum credibility. In the General Election, Fianna Fáil were returned with an overall majority of 69; Fine Gael 48, Labour 13, Independents 8. The constitution was passed by 685,105 against 526,945, being carried in thirty of the thirty-four electoral areas, the exceptions being Wicklow, Sligo, Dublin townships and Cork West.

The function of the President was to be Head of State, signing all Bills passed by Parliament, accrediting Ambassadors and could seek advice from the Council of State. The Head of the Dáil from now on was to be the Taoiseach (Prime Minister). The new Senate was to be made up of sixty members – eleven to be nominated by the Taoiseach, six to be elected by the Universities, and the rest representing various vocational, professional and cultural interests. It could suggest changes to a Bill, but could only hold a Bill up for ninety days and could not stop a Bill permanently.

Anglo-Irish Agreement

The acceptance of the Constitution was obvious when De Valera met McDonald and the only topics mentioned were partition, finance, the ports, defence and trade. De Valera's vews were strong and to the point:

[1]   End of partition.
[2]   No money to be paid for annuities.
[3]   No commitment on British use of ports in war time.
[4]   That the payments due to Britain could be written off against Ireland's refusal to be used by a foreign power against Britain.

In the meeting on 16th, McDonald stressed objections to Articles 2.13 of the constitution. De Valera stressed that no agreements or good relations could be achieved as long as partition remained. Britain said they would not stand in the way of a settlement between Ireland and the North on partition, but would not state publicly that they desired an end to partition.

Then on November 24th, 1937, on an invitation from De Valera, it was agreed that a meeting of Ministers of the two Governments would take place with a view to a final settlement, which no doubt Britain needed due to the threat of war. The agenda was to include partition, defence and finance.

In the meantime, Lord Craigavon called a General Election in the North in which the Unionists won forty-one out of the fifty-two seats, which no doubt ruled out any bargaining over partition at the Irish-British meeting.

The meeting took place at 10 Downing Street on January 17th, 1938. The Irish Ministers present were: An Taoiseach, Éamon De Valera, Seán Lemass (Industry and Commerce), Seán McEntee (Finance) and Dr. J. Ryan (Agriculture). Britain was represented by Prime Minister Neville Chamberlain, Sir John Simon (Finance), Sir Samuel Hoare (Home Secretary), Malcolm McDonald (Dominions Secretary), Sir Thomas Inskip (Defence), Oliver Shanley (Board of Trade) and W. S. Morrison (Agriculture).

The talks covered three long sessions in London. No advance was made in the question of partition. Though Chamberlain admitted to De Valera that partition was an anachronism, he was unwilling to go public on that as he felt he would not get the backing of his Cabinet colleagues. De Valera wrote to US President Roosevelt explaining that the main stumbling block to good relations with Britain was partition, and that a solution to this problem would be of major benefit, not alone to Irish-British relations at home, but in every country where these two peoples lived.

While Roosevelt would not agree to do anything publicly, he did promise that the new Ambassador to Britain, Joseph P. Kennedy, would be advised to use his influence with Chamberlain regarding a solution.

De Valera informed the British that it might be difficult to obtain a proposed defence agreement from his Cabinet colleagues if nothing could be done about partition. He made excellent headway with the question of ports, convincing the British that it would be in their interest, with war looming, to hand back the ports unencumbered – which they did.

With regards to the annuities and other payments which amounted to £104 million, De Valera was successful in getting the figure down to a £10 million, 'once off', lump sum. The £10 million would not be characterised as annuities. The trade discussions centred mostly around the duties imposed by both countries during the Economic War. These were to be finally disposed with, with a few exceptions.

Towards the end of the final session, there was almost a complete breakdown as Britain refused to budge on partition, and Ireland refused to trade concessions to Northern Ireland, as requested by Britain.

It appears that an intervention made by Joseph P. Kennedy saved the day, though the significance of Kennedy is a matter of opinion.

Anyhow, whatever caused the change of mind, Ireland signed the Anglo-Irish Agreement on April 25th, 1938, which contained the following main points –
  (1) Ireland was given back the ports, with no rights to Britain
  (2) There was to be no defence agreement with Britain
  (3) A "once-off" payment of £10 million was to end the financial dispute
  (4) No trade concessions to the 'six counties'.

De Valera was not totally happy with the outcome as he had not made any breakthrough on partition. It was to be a few years later that the people realised the great concessions given by Britain, particularly the return of the ports and the refusal to have a defence agreement with Britain. It was these points in particuar, that enabled Ireland to maintain its neutrality during the Second World War 1939-1945.

After Chamberlain's refusal to go public on his attitude to partition, the only solution De Valera could see for partition was a public relations campaign in the UK. Not too long after the Anglo-Irish Agreement, a snap vote in the Dáil on arbitration on public pay brought defeat for the Government. Fianna Fáil won the resulting election with 77 out of the 138 seats giving it a majority of 16 seats.

De Valera set out now on the public relations trail. He first brought in Liam McMahon, who had been a prominent figure in the Irish Self Determination League (1919). In an interview with the *Evening Standard*, De Valera spoke on options on partition, either an All-Ireland Parliament with PR to suit the small parties or more practically, that Belfast keep its present powers but hand over the powers that Westminster had regarding the six counties to Dublin.

Simultaneously, with De Valera launching his public relations campaign, an activist group of the IRA, having given an ultimatum for British withdrawal, began its bombing campaign in the UK. In Coventry, five people were killed and and ten people injured. These were very counter-poductive to De Valera's plan.

Another blow to his anti-partition campaign was Chamberlain's attempt to inroduce compulsory conscription in the six counties, aided and abetted by Lord Craigavon.

De Valera attacked this move in the Dáil as an act of agression and Chamberlain dropped it. Though it would be unfair to expect the Catholic Nationalist minority to fight for a Britain that seperated it from it's fellow men by a border. The decision to drop compulsory conscription was resented by the Unionists, who did not want to be treated different to mainland Britain.

Though De Valera and Chamberlain had got as close as one could wish on the partition question, the IRA outrage, the conscription case and later the neutrality question, did not endear the South to either Britain or the Unionists, nor did it, in general, help the partition question.

The War and Neutrality

One of the greatest successes of De Valera and Fianna Fáil was the way in which, against all appeals and threats from Britain, Germany and the USA and European allies, Ireland was able to remain neutral during the course of the Second World War. This was one of the most wonderful and balancing acts of diplomacy in international politics.

In adition to the external threats, De Valera also had to ensure that he had consensus in the Dáil with the opposition, as well as keeping the threat of the IRA under firm control.

Britain, under Chamberlain and later under Churchuill, put a lot of pressure on De Valera for the return of the ports and to enter the war on the side of the allies. Churchill, especially tried everthing from threat to enticement, by the promise of a United Ireland, provided the Unionists consented. De Valera stood firm. It is generally known now that several times when Britain was under pressre during the war, that Churchill had contemplated invading. He was no doubt put off doing so by the realisation that De Valera would make it an international issue and compare it to the German invasions of Poland, Belgium, Holland and others. This would negate Britain's cause for entering the war and give her bad public relations. He probably also feared that in breaching neutrality that Ireland might help Germany. Churchill knew also that he was dealing with a man of De Valera's stature who could be relied on not to accept it sitting down. As well as that, De Valera had been taking precautions for an invasion by strengthening the army, destroying certain archives and transporting the gold reserves from Dublin to Foynes.

However, De Valera was able to maintain friendly relations with Britain, turning a blind eye to crashed British pilots returning over the border, thousands of Irish joining the British Army, thousands of others working in British factories and hospitals, as well as offering refuge to women and children from air raid areas in Ireland. He also had allowed meetings between British army officers in the North with army officers in the South.

Other notable co-operation between De Valera and Britain recorded in O'Neill's and Lord Longford's biography of De Valera were, "instant reporting and signalling, the acceptance of naval attaché and wide facilities for investigation, the holding up at Maffey's request for a series of emergency orders, implementing neutrality in detail, the retention of the Admiralty Tug at Cobh [and] the fact that British surface craft would pursue and attack hostile submarines in the territorial waters of Ireland".

Anthony Eden, foreign secretary, was working with three options in dealing with De Valera:

(1) More dialogue with De Valera, re: getting the ports.

(2) Acquiesce with De Valera and get small concessions.

(3) Forcibly use harbours.

In the end, he and British policy opted for the second option.

On the home front, De Valera had to deal with certain elements who looked on Britain's dilemma as Ireland's opportunity. The IRA linked up with certain Germans who felt that they could be a help in the defeat of Britain. De Valera responded with some of the toughest measures ever, under the Offences Against the State act of 1939. Over 1,000 IRA men were jailed or interned, six were executed and three others died on hunger strike, but he knew from sad experience that, by giving in to one, the consequences would be so widespread that he had no alternative. About twelve other IRA men and twelve detectives lost their lives in action. De Valera had also advised Hempel, the German Ambassador, that Germany's involvement with the IRA would not help Ireland's future relationship with Germany. Hempel relayed this message to Germany and the threat died away. It was also possible of course, that the IRA involvement with Germany would give Britain the excuse to invade Ireland.

At the same time, De Valera showed his firmness with Germany. He protested vehemently at the "cruel wrong" of Germany's invasion of Holland and Belgium. He objected strongly after the German bombing of Dublin. He took a chance by sending the Dublin Fire Brigade service to Belfast after the Germans had bombed the city. He inisisted on a radio transmitter in the German Embassy being handed over to the Irish Government. On the other hand he paid a formal call to the German Legate on the death of Hitler to pay his condolences. On criticism from Churchill for this, he retorted by saying, "not to do so would be an act of unpardonable discourtesy to the German people".

The American Minister in Ireland at the beginning of the war was John Cudahy, who, being of Kilkenny extract was sympathetic with Ireland's neutrality. However, the American point of view to Ireland's neutrality seemed to change drastically when David Gray was appointed Minister in April 1944. Gray's attitude was very pro-British and he was pushing for the use of the Irish ports. The Irish minister in the US, Bob Brennan, met Sumner Welles, Under-Secretary of the State Department and found that he agreed with Ireland's position of neutrality, though Gray later disagreed with Brennan's version of the meeting. In addition, David Gray was castigating De Valera as a martyr, fanatic and Machiavellian and though neither pro-German not Anti-British, to be pro-De Valera.

At a time that the British position was getting more critical and with Churchill getting more anxious over the non-use of the Irish ports, Gray was busy setting up pro-British elements in Ireland to force Ireland into the war, while at the same time, the US itself remained neutral.

Churchill decided that as Ireland would not budge, he could cut off supplies of essential items like oil and tea and use their ships for the war purposes. De Valera's earlier policy of self-sufficency, however, was to be of great benefit to the country now, together with his decision to buy his own ships.

A statement made by De Valera that the belligerents, "in blockading each other are blockading us" and Aiken being misrepresented in the US, led to an angry meeting of Gray and De Valera. Gray was accusing Ireland of being critical of his America attitude which is what Gray himself was doing in Ireland – trying to turn the opposition against De Valera. In addition, Gray offered two ships to De Valera, instead of through the proper channels to Aiken. De Valera refused the offer. De Valera was utterly loyal to his cabinet colleagues. De Valera did, however, get the ships he wanted and they became the *Irish Oak* and the *Irish Pine* of the fleet of Irish Shipping Ltd., a state-sponsored company set up in March 1941. The fleet was later increased to eight and this countered the British decision not to send supplies to Ireland. They became vital for the shipping of goods to Ireland throughout the war and in helping Ireland's neutrality.

An attempt by Churchill at this time to introduce conscription in the North was thwarted by a combination of interventions by Cardinal McRory in Armagh, David Gray, Dulanty and De Valera, on the basis "that it would produce the bitterest resentment amongst Irishmen and would have the most disastrous consequences for our two peoples".

Other events of note during the war years included the setting up of the Department of Supplies under Seán Lemass in 1939. It was here, with the help of John Leydon, Secretary of the Department, and his most talented team of Civil Servants, that Lemass really began to show his organisational ability, giving his team sufficient scope and cutting through red tape.

As war was imminent, De Valera having taken into account the plight of small nations within the League of Nations decided that neutrality was the best option. It was evident to him in the League that the great powers dominated; not giving the smaller nations any say in war or peace and this was why we were facing a war now.

In choosing neutrality, he was certain to have to deal with many factors and this was how it was. He had to use his greatest diplomacy in dealing with Britain, Germany and the USA, as well as opposition in the Dáil and the IRA

With regard to Germany, Dr Hempel, the German minister in Dublin, had a meeting with De Valera and promised him that Germany would respect Irish neutrality. The next day, Hitler invaded Poland, In the Dáil, while De Valera showed sympathy to Poland, he reiterated that as six of our counties were held under aggression by England, we had to put our own dilemma first. This was accepted by the opposition.

Lemass was appointed head of a new Department of Supplies. It was now obvious that the policy of Protectionism and self-sufficiency was to be a major advantage.

At this time, Britain did not have a representative as such in Dublin, which would make communications with London very difficult during war-time. It was eventually agreed that Sir John Maffey would be posted in Dublin with the title of "Representative to Dublin".

Seán Lemass

If the first leader of Fianna Fáil was of Spanish decent on his father's side, the second leader could be described as of French descent. In the late 17th century, French Huguenots under religious persecution from Catholic France fled their native country to England, Scotland and Ireland. One Scottish family named Le Maistre came to settle in Armagh in 1820, and started a clothing business there. They later moved to Dublin.

By 1845 the name Le Maistee had become Lemass. Seán Lemass' grandfather opened a hatter's business in No. 2, Capel Street in 1867. His father, John Lemass continued the business and lived over the shop in his early married life. Noel Lemass, Seán's eldest brother, was born there in 1897. As the business expanded, John Lemass and his wife moved to a house in Ballybrack, where the future Taoiseach was born on 15th July 1899.

As a young boy, he attended Holy Faith College, Haddington Road, transferring at the age of nine to O'Connell's CBS, Richmond Street. By the time he obtained a first class distinction in his Inter Cert in 1915, and had gone to Rosses College, he had already become a member of "A" company of the 3rd battalion of the Volunteers, being introduced by one of his father's employees, Pat Mullen. Although he was still six months short of an acceptable age, he was accepted as Pat Mullen told him that he looked "a bit older" and it would only be a "little white lie anyway".

Shortly after this, De Valera became Battalion Commandant and Lemass was appointed his personal aide.

It was not to be long before Lemass became involved in very active service – in fact the 1916 insurrection. He was aware in advance of the 1916 rising and the following is his own description of his involvement in it, as he described in an article of "Studies", (1966 Spring Edition).

> "On Easter Monday, 1916, my elder brother Noel and I, having had no orders or information about what was going to happen since Professor MacNeill's cancellation of the Parade of Volunteers on Easter Sunday, went for a walk in the Dublin mountains with our friends, Jim and Ken O'Dea. We walked to Glencree and returned in the afternoon. I was then seventeen years of age and my brother nineteen.

> "Around 5pm and some distance outside Rathfarnham, we met Professor MacNeill and two of his sons riding on bicycles

outwards from the city. We had a slight acquaintance with the MacNeill boys and they dismounted and spoke to us. It was from them that we first learnt of the Rising.

"Professor MacNeill seemed agitated and depressed. He informed us that the Volunteers had occupied various positions in the city, but that he had had no information as to further events. He was very clearly unhappy about the whole situation.

"There were no trams running from Rathfarnam so we had to walk into the city. We went to Jacob's factory which was the first position occupied by the Volunteers which we came to, but the windows were barricaded and we could make no contact with the defenders.

"Noel and I got up early the next morning, and with no word from our parents, left home determined to take part in the Rising. We went first to the Four Courts, which was the position nearest to our home in Capel Street, where we were informed that our own unit, the Third Battalion, was in the Ringsend direction. We decided to make our way there, but when passing the GPO we met a friend, Volunteer Hugh Holohan, on sentry duty and he brought us inside where we were absorbed into the garrison and given arms.

"Noel was despatched across the street to the Imperial Hotel, where he was wounded in the subsequent fighting. I was sent to a position on the roof of the GPO at the corner nearest the Pillar, where there was a group of eight or ten Volunteers, including a couple of Citizen Army men, under the command of a Volunteer Officer named Cremin who had come from London to take part in the Rising.

"At this position on the roof there were a number of rather crude bombs made out of billy-cans and equipped with slow-burning fuses. The idea was that, in the case of a mass assault on the GPO, we were to light the fuses and throw them on the attackers in the street below.

"We remained in position on the roof until Thursday, when we were ordered down from the building. The stage of serious fighting was beginning at the GPO and there was tremendous activity inside preparing for the attack which was assumed to be pending. Later on that day, the shelling started, and activity was directed to fire-fighting, although the initial damage done by the exploding shells was surprisingly light.

"The shelling continued on Friday and late on that day as the building became well alight, the word went around that its evacuation was to begin. O'Rahilly and his men had made their gallant but ill-fated charge up Moore Street and it had been decided to work up this street by tunnelling through the houses so that another charge on the British barricade at the Parnell Street end of it would be attempted. We were given to understand that the general objective was to occupy a new position in Williams and Woods factory in Parnell Street.

"Many people have claimed to have helped in carrying the wounded Connolly from the GPO. In fact, the process was so slow and so frequently interrupted that almost everyone in the GPO helped in at some stage and personally, I assisted to carry Connolly's stretcher for a short distance to a small door opening on Henry Street, where however, I was ordered, with all those around, to proceed at the run up the small back street, Moore Lane opposite the GPO.

"Another back street running parallel to Moore Street intersected this, and down this a continuous flow of machine-gun and rifle fire poured. Those who were first across the intersection, of whom I was one, escaped unharmed but some of the main body following us were killed or wounded here.

"A house at the corner of Moore Street was entered and all that night relays of men tunnelled through the walls up the street. Moore Street was littered with dead people, including some of the Volunteers who died in the O'Rahilly charge and, much more numerous, men, woman and children who had tried to leave their homes. The next day the tunnelling process ended in a warehouse yard not very far from the British barricade. Those volunteers who possessed bayonets for their rifles, of whom I was one, were directed to this yard and I arrived there when various obstacles which had been blocking the doorway were being quietly removed, so that the way would be cleared for us to pour out in the intended charge.

"During the week I had eaten very little and slept hardly at all. Surprisingly enough however, while waiting in the yard, I experienced both hunger and fatigue. I ate a tin of preserved fruit from a shop through which we had passed, and while seated on the stairway into the yard, watching the obstacles being removed, I fell asleep for a few moments.

"When I awoke, Seán McDermott had come into the yard and had

*begun to address us, to tell us of the decision to surrender. He
spoke briefly but very movingly and many of those present were
weeping. Some time after he had departed, we were paraded in
single column and marched out of the yard into Moore Street,
headed by Captain M.W. O'Reilly and a Volunteer bearing a white
flag. We marched back up Moore Street into Henry Street, which
was littered with debris from the burning and destroyed buildings,
and into O'Connell Street.*

*"In O'Connell Street, under the guns of the British military lining
the street, we laid down our arms. We spent that night in the open,
crowded into the gardens outside the Rotunda, and were marched
the next morning, in long column under guard, to Richmond
Barracks in Inchicore".*

In December 1920, Lemass was arrested and imprisoned in
Ballykinnear (Co. Down). It was during this year that he began to learn
economics, which was to serve him and the nation well with his famous
economic plan which was to begin to transform Ireland from a 19th
Century Agricultural Economy to a 20th Century Modern Industrial
state.

He was released from Ballykinnear after the signing of the Treaty.
He became training officer for the new Irish Police Force, but resigned
on the receipt of his first pay cheque, as it was drawn on the provisional
government. That, plus the fact that the Treaty contained the Oath of
Allegiance and Partition played no small part in him going back to
Beggars Bush as Training Officer of the anti-Treaty forces.

Shortly afterwards, under the command of Paddy O'Brien, they
occupied the Four Courts, the beginning of the Civil War. On the
surrender of the Four Courts, they were arrested, but Lemass and Ernie
O'Malley managed to escape from a yard where they were being held,
and having tried and failed to link up with Andy McDonnell's Brigade,
they linked up with a Tipperary Brigade at Blessington and marched
southwards to Wexford, where they helped to capture Ferns and
Enniscorthy from the Free State Troops.

Due to some confusion here, they returned to Baltinglass and were
lucky to escape capture, having been surrounded by Free State Troops.
Lemass and Tom Derrig then proceeded to walk all the way back to
Dublin. Shortly afterwards, Lemass was appointed Second in Command
to Ernie O'Malley for the Eastern Command.

In December 1922, he was captured by the Free State Troops and
was interned at the Curragh where he was subjected to the most extreme

torture, especially after an escape tunnel which he was masterminding was discovered. He was rather lucky to escape execution, as attempting to escape was then a capital offence. Probably the announcement of the ceasefire by De Valera saved his life.

Then came the tragic news that his brother Noel's body had been found murdered in the Dublin Mountains. He was released for the funeral in October 1923. He then returned to his father's business in Capel Street and married Kathleen Hughes. His best man was Jimmy O'Dea, the actor.

Defeat in the Civil War began to change the thinking of the anti-Treaty forces towards the political plane. In the Sinn Féin Ard Fheis of 1923, Lemass was elected on to the Standing Committee of the Party. Though still an army man, at heart, with the IRA now in decline he found himself being pulled more and more towards politics. As an organiser, Lemass showed his skills in many of the committees he was on, and he found himself to the forefront of organising many events, especially Easter Sunday commemorations.

The high esteem in which Lemass was held now can be established by the fact that he was selected as a candidate in the South Dublin constituency, due to the death of Philip Cosgrave. He was however, unsuccessful in this attempt. A second election in the same constituency not long after, caused by the appointment of Hugh Kennedy from Attorney General to Chief Justice, proved successful.

In and around 1925 he published articles in the party's paper, *An Phoblacht*, which criticised many of the policies of the party, suggesting that the party would be better off focusing on immediate issues like the Oath of Allegiance. As rumours were circulating that the Republican Government were considering entering the Dáil, the army broke away from them.

Then, between December 1925 and August 1926, three major things occurred that were to speed up the process of a new party being formed, and that party taking their seats in Dáil Éireann. On December 3rd, the Boundary Agreement was signed, giving more or less full recognition to partition. Attempts by Sinn Féin deputies to link up with Labour and enter the Dáil to defeat the agreement failed. This had a major bearing on Lemass and De Valera, as they saw the disadvantages of being on the outside, due to their abstentionist policy.

At the Sinn Féin Ard Fheis on March 9, 926, De Valera proposed *"... that once the admission oaths of the twenty-six county assembly are removed, it becomes a question of policy, rather than principle whether or not republican representatives should attend these assemblies."* A countermotion by Fr. O'Flanagan was carried by a small majority. De Valera resigned as President and left the hall, accompanied by Lemass and a substantial number of others. He alluded to Lemass, "that was that", and that he was leaving politics altogether. It was then that Lemass put to him the idea of forming a new party.

A few weeks later, the new party was formed and Seán Lemass became Joint Secretary with Gerry Boland. There was a dispute as to what the name of the party would be with De Valera proposing Fianna Fáil and Lemass proposing the Republican Party. A compromise was arrived at with the party being called Fianna Fáil, followed by 'The Republican Party'.

On November 24th, 1926, Fianna Fail held its first Ard Fheis in La Scala theatre, attended by fifty delegates. De Valera was appointed President and Seán Lemass, along with Gerry Boland, became Joint Secretaries on a full-time basis.

Now the real job at organising the new party began. Lemass travelled up and down the country in a baby Ford car, putting together the base of what was to become the biggest party in the country to this present day. He visited all his old Sinn Féin and IRA colleagues that he could trust and they helped him to set up Cumainn, and a constituency organisation all over the country. By 1932 there were 1,000 branches. As he went around the country, he found that though a majority had defeated De Valera's proposals at the Sinn Féin Ard Fheis in 1925, this feeling was not reflected in the country.

The success of the organising of the party was another proof of the enormous organising ability which Seán Lemass had shown to date, but gave one an idea of what he would do in the future. However, it was not the only talent he had, and he also played a significant part in the formulation of party policy.

Another factor, which speeded up the entering of the Dáil for the Deputies, was the assassination of Kevin O'Higgins, Minister for Justice and External Affairs in the Cumman na nGaedhal Government on July 10th, 1927. This led to the introduction of the Electoral Amendment Bill on August 10th. The idea of this Bill was to disqualify Deputies who refused to take the Oath of Allegiance. That night Fianna Fáil held a meeting. Lemass and Boland pushed for the party entering the Dáil and were successful. The next day, Fianna Fáil entered the Dáil.

Within a few days of entering the Dáil, Fianna Fáil and Labour would have toppled the Government on a vote of no confidence were it not for Sligo Labour T. D., Deputy Binks, being unable to be present for the vote, due to a large dose of intoxicating liquor from his Cumman na nGaedhal friends.

Cumman na nGaedhal, realising their marginal position, called a General Election for September 15th. They managed to increase their majority with the following results: - Cumman na nGaedhal 62 + 15 (30.4%), Fianna Fail 57 + 13, and the other parties being decimated.

The next five years were a great sabbatical for Fianna Fáil, giving them time to adjust to parliamentary procedures. Lemass being a full-time politician enabled him to be a spokesman for economic affairs and a foremost formulation of policy and direction for the party. By the time the next election came, they were more than ready to take up the reigns of government.

The young Lemass in opposition was recognised as, on the one hand, Republican, with political agitation still in reserve, to, as he described himself, "slightly constitutional". He was well able to bear a militant attitude on one hand, with attacks on the Government for their police harassment and ill-treatment of prisoners under the guise of the Public Safety Act. On the other hand, he was gaining a formidable reputation as the spokesman for Economics and Public Finance.

He constantly attacked the Government on their inaction, accusing them of "driving the industrial car with a foot on the brake, rather than on the accelerator". The unemployment problem, he maintained, needed an emergency plan on a national basis, building up the home economy by fiscal policies that would tax capital being exported with a tax relief on Irish money being invested in Ireland. He was a firm believer in an interventionist social and economic policy, but only when industry is depressed and unemployment is high.

Lemass, the city man, though admitting that he knew little of farming, blamed the Government for causing emigration from the land with their "policy of allowing the farmers to do what they liked with the land, regardless of their effect on the community". He maintained that "unless the system of using the land is altered, so that more employment can be provided on it, and industries started that will give occupation to surplus population on the land, were likely to have periods of depression recurring frequently."

Lemass in his economic thinking was influenced on the one hand by Arthur Griffith's old Sinn Féin Policies, but he was also influenced by international trends that were getting more protectionist at the time.

A world depression, drop in prices and public service pay, an increase in the closure of factories, and unemployment all helped towards a change of Government. The General Election took place on February 16, 1932, and the results were as follows: - Fianna Fáil 72 seats, +15 (43.7%), Cumman na nGaedhal 57 seats, - 5 (35.3%). Fianna Fail had now become the largest party in Dáil Éireann, a position they have never lost to date.

With the help of Labour, De Valera was appointed President, and Seán Lemass became Minister for Industry and Commerce, one on the most important portfolio's of the day, as it encompasses Labour, Social Welfare, Transport & Power (which are major departments in their own right in later years). At 33 years of age, he was the youngest minister in Europe.

On entering the Dáil, Fianna Fáil felt tense, as they reckoned the Cosgrave regime would not hand over power easily. It was rumoured that some Fianna Fáil Deputies had their pockets bulging with guns. Whether there is any truth in that or not, such precautions were not necessary and power was handed over quietly.

Very quickly after getting into power, Lemass introduced protective tariffs on a large number of produce. This, together with the Economic War with Britain, enabled Lemass to establish industries, and in the next four years increased employment by 43,000, mostly in manufacturing.

He also established Aer Lingus and the Sugar Company in this period, which prompted the famous British Economist, John M. Keys to express at a guest lecture in U.C.D. in 1933 that, *"If I were an Irishman, I would find much to attract me in the economic outlook of your present Government towards greater self-sufficiency"*.

With his Social Welfare hat, he introduced unemployment assistance, widow's and orphan's pensions, and children's allowance.

Another of Lemass' achievements was his motivation of his fellow ministers and civil servants. Foremost in Lemass's plans at this time was Secretary of the Department of Finance – John Leydon.

In his first day as Minister he got straight down to work. His first decision was to appoint John Leydon as Secretary of the Department. Leydon, at the time, was a senior civil servant of note and had turned down an invitation by W.T. Cosgrave to take up that position on the basis that it might be unacceptable to the new Government. He also informed Lemass that he did not agree with all his ideas, to which Lemass stated that he did not want a 'Yes Man'. As head of his Department, Leydon gave his Senior Staff the choice to resign or stay.

Three of the stipulations of Labour supporting Fianna Fáil in Government were:-
(1) Protectionism
(2) Reduce Unemployment
(3) Developing indigenous resources.

In 1932 he introduced the Customs Duties (Provisional Imposition) Act, 1932, and three Finance Acts to protect a large number of products. On the outbreak of the Economic War, he introduced the Emergency Imposition of Duty Act, 1932, to negate preferential treatment given to British and Commonwealth imports.

On June 8th, he implemented the Control of Manufacturing Bill, which required manufacturers to obtain a new manufacturers licence for a new manufacturing business, such licences not being available to non-nationals.

Lemass was one of a cabinet committee headed by De Valera, set up "to examine and report on the economic conditions..." for the Imperial Economic Conference in July 1932. Recommendations that came from this committee approved by Government were:
(1) Heavy expenditure on Roads and Houses.
(2) Trade Loans (Guarantee) Act to Building Schemes.
(3) An Industrial Development Branch in the Department of Industry & Commerce.
(4) Registry for the Unemployed.

Attending at a conference in Ottawa to develop a Commonwealth Free Trade Area, where he failed to secure preferential treatment for Irish Exports, he was informed there that Britain had imposed tariffs in retaliation to the Government's refusal to pay the land annuities due to Britain. He immediately wrote a letter from Ottawa to De Valera, recommending counteraction, stating that it could be turned to our advantage if people were willing to suffer short-term for long-term benefits.

As regards the Commonwealth, Lemass maintained that if we were not getting any benefits from our membership, we would be as well out of it. By the autumn of 1932, the Economic War was taking its toll and Lemass suggested drastic measures to prevent the state from "collapse".

The situation required drastic action, and Lemass had any number of proposals to put before the Executive Council, which were: cuts in expenditure (including education), nationalisation of essential imports (to be purchased and re-sold at a small profit), a Board to control external trade (including agriculture), reduce agricultural production, remove surplus people from the land, curtail agricultural profits, a major public works scheme, speed up industrial development, reduce imports, establish industrial and agricultural marketing organisations, abolish land annuities, found a state bank, found an industrial credit organisation and separate Irish currency from Sterling.

This was quite a list and was obviously not going to get through in full or fast. In addition, he put two further proposals in a letter to De Valera which were: legislation to prevent the unemployed from being evicted (even by a Local Authority), and weekly unemployment assistance.

The Executive Council met on November 18th, 1932, and looking at all the proposals some were passed, some scrapped, some deferred and some postponed. The proposal to prevent evictions was quickly rejected, while the Unemployment Assistance idea was dispatched to the Department of Finance. Jim Ryan, Minister for Agriculture, knocked the bid to control External Trade on the head. The plan to take people from the land was opposed by Finance's J.J. Mc Elligott, who believed it would be wrong to take people who's only experience was farming and put them out to wait for Industrial Development, that was still only a dream.

Lemass, hampered in some areas, always had the determination to succeed in another direction, and it was not too long until he had set up the Control of Manufacturers Act 1932 – 1934. (October 29th 1932), and the Industrial Credit Corporation (1933).

This, together with the earlier Custom Duties & Finance Act, helped to create the framework for industrial development. Other legislation encompassed the Agricultural Price Support, social Legislation (on unemployment and conditions of work), and a policy for building houses contributed to Lemass's overall plan.

Though according to Garrett Fitzgerald in his book, *Planning in Ireland*, that there was *"no rational basis"* to the implementation of tariffs, yet Lemass succeeded and induced industries to set up behind the tariff walls which helped to increase employment in the manufacturing industry by 43,000 between 1931 and 1936. During all this time, he was often playing a lone hand, as many of his colleagues in Cabinet did not agree with his policies. This was specifically apparent when he was introducing his Control of Manufacturers Act, as he was forced to re-draft it and was left with the barest minimum required.

As local manufacturers looked to the Protection Policy, they now, in a series of meeting asked Lemass to improve on it, by not eliminating foreign competition, but by preventing entry to local industry where manufacturing had needed separation.

An amendment Bill in 1934 went some of the way, stopping short where it might cause large implications. There was some disagreement about decentralisation of industry at this time, as all new industries were going to Dublin.

The Factories Protection Act was used by Lemass to protect indigenous industry with native organisations and capital, and only permit outside business in, which could not be satisfied by native enterprise. Outside industries, which had been established beforehand, often lost out to indigenous industries as Ranks, who had in 1933 a third of the milling market did ; by 1936, Irish Mills had gained a 100% share of the Irish Market.

Other foreign companies who, by law, could not get around the act, were also discouraged, like for example, Hovis, who Lemass scared off with the threat of 2d per pound excise duties.

Cement was an industry that was exempt from the Act, and Lemass induced SALTS – the UK spinning company to fill that void in the Free State Economy. Dunlop was another company that was persuaded to come, and unlike other companies setting up in Dublin, it eventually agreed to open in Cork.

Due to too many demands being made by Labour towards the end of 1932, De Valera, on the supposed advice of Lemass, called a surprise General Election to dissolve the partnership. Fianna Fáil's Manifesto promised to cut Land Annuities by 50% and introduces policies to help the poor. This election saw the emergence of the Centre Party. Fianna Fáil, with some behind the scenes help from the IRA, won their first overall majority with 49.7% of the vote, giving them 77 seats. Cumman na nGaedhal got 30.5% with 48 seats, Labour 5.7% with 8 seats, the Centre Party 9.1% with 11 seats and Independents 5%, with 9 seats.

With the party now firmly in power, Lemass proceeded with even more conviction to implement his Economic Policy, industrially and agriculturally. The policies put forward for Agriculture did not stop the flow of the people towards the urban areas. It has been agreed by many, even Lemass's closest colleagues, that he lacked a sense of rural needs and was basically as 'city man'. All the progress he was making met with a conservative bias in the Cabinet, which was a hindrance to him, especially in the persons of McEntee (Finance), Senator Joseph

Connelly, (Post & Telegraphs), and Aiken in Foreign Affairs. However, it would appear at all stages that he had the backing of De Valera, even though his objectives were more of a patriotic nature. At one stage, De Valera stated that Lemass was his "most brilliant Minister". 1937 was again a General Election year and Fianna Fáil went back to power with the help of Labour. This was the year when De Valera put the new Constitution before the people. Lemass's advice to De Valera was that the constitution should not be a Manifesto of "Fianna Fáil's Social policy". The Constitution was carried. In 1938, Labour pulled the plug over a disagreement about Civil Servant's pay, and caused a General Election. Fianna Fáil were again returned to power with an overall majority with 77 seats. In this period Lemass carried on, and despite Cabinet (Executive) resistance he created and developed a number of Semi-State bodies such as the Industrial Credit Company, Bord na Mona and Irish Life Assurance. In 1936, Lemass initiated what he later stated to be his finest achievement – Aer Lingus, with a capital of £100,000. During this period also, he introduced improvements in Social Welfare such as Widow's Pensions. He had got built 130,000 houses, had improved health services, and the State's acceptance that the problem of unemployment had to be recognised.

By 1938 Lemass felt that the Economic War was becoming a major stumbling block to economic progress. He had, in 1934, achieved some progress in opening up trade with the coal-for-cattle pact and a similar deal in 1936 with the cement-for-cattle pact. In January 1938 a team made up of De Valera, Lemass, McEntee and Dr. Ryan went to London to discuss with their counterparts the ending of the Economic War and the negotiation of what was to become the Anglo-Irish Agreement of 1938. The primary benefits of this agreement were as follows: -
  (1) Free entry into the UK market (with some limitations for Irish industrial goods).
  (2) Ireland maintaining its protective barriers.
  (3) Equal access for Irish and British farmers.
  (4) Return of the ports.

The next major event in 1938 was the Report of the Commission on Banking. A Commission on Banking had been established in 1926 but it resulted in no change being made. A new Commission was set up in 1934 "to report in 1938 to examine... the system... of Currency, Banking, Credit, Public Borrowing and Lending and pledging State Credit... to ... Agriculture and Industry". This Commission again decided in (1) no changes as to Parity with Sterling, (2) Tight control on Semi-State borrowing, (3) Establishment of a Currency Commission to act as a Central Bank. This did eventually lead to the passing of the Central Bank Act 1942. Lemass's idea of a Central Bank was to have the power to control and influence the Credit operation within the country; when to allow the commercial banks to increase loans or if the climate changed to have the power to compel the commercial banks to decrease loans. This led to some hassle between Lemass and the Department of Finance, including the new Minister, Seán T. O'Kelly.

Lemass also attempted to set up an Irish Oil Refinery which would enjoy a monopoly. Again he met with objections, not alone form the opposition, but the old resistance within his own party of McEntee, Senator Connelly and even the Attorney General. Their main objections were (1) Redundancy of workers engaged in existing refineries, (2) Pollution. Having got Cabinet approval, he entered into an agreement with Thames Oil Water Company, who in turn were coerced out of the project by Shell. Though shipping magnate Andrew Weir stepped in, instead of Thames Oil And Water Company, the war eventually intervened and Lemass's talents were to be channelled elsewhere – in the Department of Supplies.

De Valera described Lemass's position as catering for 'the central planning development of our economic life". Lemass wanted to continue the 'emergency' system of central economic planning after the war but it must have met with Cabinet opposition as it never happened until Jack Lynch and Martin O'Donoghue introduced a Department of Economic Planning in 1977.

Due I suppose, to the world depression of the early 30's and indeed the fear of the oncoming war, there was a secret departmental committee of civil servants in place from 1935 onwards, so it made it seem easier now to translate it into a full department. But an easy job it was not, as Lemass found out. Though he got co-operation from industrialists, he met with little help form the Federation of Irish manufacturers, the banks or the oil distributors. Added to that he got no co-operation from McEntee with regard to insuring property against war damage. He had to insure Irish ships with the British Board of Trade. In Frank Gallagher's notes on Lemass he states that "He sheltered the Irish people from the worst shortages and, where imported goods could not be got, a native substitute was developed and used in its place". Vincent Browne mentions in an article in *Nusight* in October 1969 that "Lemass decided that a job was to be done urgently and efficiently and he wasn't going to be bound by official red tape or outmoded civil service tradition . . . they kept the minimum of files . . . Paperwork was reduced to a minimum". In 1941 Lemass set up Irish Shipping with fifteen vessels purchased abroad or commandeered at home to ensure that Ireland could get essential supplies into the country. This came about after Britain broke an agreement to charter ships to the Irish Government at the beginning of the war. This was on account of Ireland not giving over the ports to fight the war.

Though the job that Lemass did in the war years was excellent, it did not go without that old jealous and begrudging streak that seems to haunt the country when one is successful. A vicious rumour was put out by the opposition and some within his own party about Lemass's gambling and corruption in supplies. This slander could be easily counteracted by the fact that Lemass returned chests of tea and jewellery received as presents, stating that if the Irish people had to suffer, so should his family. Another source of criticism came from the report of the Commission on Vocational Organization, chaired by Dr. Michael Brown, Bishop of Galway. On hindsight, looking at the type of mentality that Lemass was dealing with at that time, it really shows the tremendous leadership qualities he had, to overcome the narrow-mindedness that existed and being able to bring Ireland from a 19th century rural community into a modern 20th century State.

Other State-sponsored bodies set up by Lemass at that time were Bord na Móna, Chemici Teo and the Irish Sugar Company. He also introduced children's allowances, even against the wishes of the Minister for Finance, McEntee, and got the Transport Bill passed.

Development was difficult after the war. Though unemployment stood at 70,000, an expected increase from returning and demobilised soldiers did not materialise as emigration played a major part in containing the number of people out of work. 1946 saw rationing of bread, butter and fuel, and taxes had to be imposed to finance food subsidies. Fianna Fáil's version of the post-war difficulties were on record as "very different conditions faced the Fianna Fáil Government in the post-war years. An impoverished world, shortages of machinery and materials and inflated currencies were big obstacles to the resumption of national progress ,but planning and preparations went on . . . by 1947 the worst effects had passed . . . plans for industrial expansion and agricultural development, carefully prepared by the Fianna Fáil Government during the Emergency years were beginning to be put into operation".

However, in 1948, after being fifteen years in Government, things were beginning to go wrong. With high prices, a wages freeze, rationing, a severe supplementary budget, a worsening balance of payments, together with alleged scandals surrounding the take-over of the Great Southern Railway, a bacon factory and Locke's distillery were not helping Fianna Fáil's cause. Tribunals later vindicated Fianna Fáil from any of the allegations. In February 1948 De Valera, seeing that Labour was split and having been promised support from the National Labour Party, thought the time was ripe for a General Election. National Labour however, went with the opposition to defeat Fianna Fáil and form an Inter-Party Government with John A. Costello as Taoiseach. This election saw the emergence of Clann na Poblachta, a new party that had won two Bye-elections under the leadership of Seán McBride and did well in the Local Elections of 1947. The official result of the Election was: Fine Gael 31, Labour 14, National Labour 5, Independents 12, Clann na Poblachta 10, Clann na Talún 7. After the election De Valera and Frank Aiken embarked on a world tour. Lemass was left very much to carry the can on his own at home, which involved revamping the party. that had got very complacent over sixteen years of Government. He was also kept busy as Managing Director of the *Irish Press*. During this time also he launched *The Sunday Press*. This reiterates the old adage of 'give a job to a busy man'. During the period out of office, De Valera showed his management and leadership skills in action, doing a wonderful job of encouraging and restraining Lemass as well as dealing with the rest of the Cabinet, especially McEntee, Aiken and Connolly, who were often at odds with Lemass. Lemass had to put up with their conservatism and restraint and yet he achieved most of the aims he aspired to – his goals. He would not be able to achieve all these if he took the reins himself. On the election of Seán T. Kelly as President, De Valera showed the kind of respect he had for Lemass by appointing him Deputy Leader. This was not liked by the old guard who, no doubt, had eyes on the position themselves. From 1936 onwards Lemass had being trying to develop and make more efficient the Irish industrial sector, some of who had been "waxing fat on profits . . . the direct outcome of Protective Tariffs". Attempts to introduce a Foreign Trade Corporation (1946), a Trade Advisory Board (1947) and an Industrial Efficiency Bill all failed to materialise and created some friction between Lemass and some industrialists. Dan Morrissey, the Minister now in Lemass's Department of Industry and Commerce, though described as a 'bull in a china shop', did in fact establish the IDA. "to advise and assist the Government in the intensification of industrial development . . .". Though it seemed like a move that would be welcome by Lemass, he criticised it. It is often felt that his reason for doing so was that he did not like Morrissey, who he thought was..."degrading Industry & Commerce", plus the fact that he was trying to make up to the industrialists he had offended with his own attempts to control them while in Government. Apart from the establishment of the IDA, the other two occurrences of note in the Inter-Party Government were: -

(1) The declaring of a Republic by John A. Costello in Ottawa in September of 1948 and
(2) The Mother and Child Scheme which brought down the Government.

The Mother and Child Scheme, which was a reactivation and expansion of a Fianna Fáil plan originally initiated by Dr. Jim Ryan, Dr. Noel Browne's idea was a scheme "giving a free health service to pregnant mothers and post-natal care for the mother and child up to the age of 16".

Objections from the Roman Catholic hierarchy and the medical profession brought about a situation whereby Dr. Browne was abandoned by his own Government colleagues and precipitated a fall of the Inter-Party Government in May 1951. Though it was thought that it was a Church v State battle, this was by no means the only reason why the government fell as cracks had appeared in the 'Coalition of Incompatibilities' long before the Mother and Child debate.

The resultant General Election saw the following returns: Fianna Fail 69, Fine Gael 40, Labour 16, Clann na Poblachta 2, Clann na Talún 6, Independents 14. With the help of the Independents and Dr Browne, (later to become a member of Fianna Fáil) Fianna Fáil were again back in Government. Lemass was again back in Industry & Commerce and was also Tánaiste, with McEntee in Finance. It was not a good time for Fianna Fáil as they were faced in 1952 with a Balance of Payments deficit of £62 million, emigration at its highest level, a major unemployment problem and slow growth. As De Valera's eyesight deteriorated he was no longer able to offer leadership. Lemass was obviously at this time playing a waiting game. This must have been further frustrated by Seán T. O'Kelly's decision to take a second term as President, which further delayed any chance that De Valera might go to the Park. Lemass never showed any animosity towards De Valera and always remained his loyal servant. This term was Fianna Fáil's worst period in office.

In this period a watered-down version of the Health Act that had brought the previous Government down was introduced by Dr. Ryan, under the watchful eye of Lemass, who was receiving advice from De Valera who was in an eye hospital in Utrecht. De Valera advised Lemass to avoid any snags. A few concessions, including a means test, were introduced and the amended Bill satisfied the hierarchy, the Medical Association and Dr. Brown, who was now supporting the Government. De Valera had also found out, through the offices of the Irish Ambassador to the Vatican, Joseph Walsh, that the theological opinion in Rome did not support the Irish bishop's stance. This ammunition was another factor in getting the Bill through the Oireachtas. In 1954 the Government fell and in the ensuing General Election Fianna Fáil lost four seats and the country again had another Inter-Party Government under John A. Costello as Taoiseach and William Norton (Labour) as Tánaiste and Minister for Industry & Commerce.

Lemass, now with time on his hands, studied the situation for future years. Having read up on an economic plan in vogue in Italy at that time, he began to put together the bones of an economic plan for Ireland which he published in the *Irish Press* in 1955 and launched at Clery's ballroom in 1956. It contained an investment plan of £67 million of public monies and private investment with the aim of creating a thousand jobs in the private sector. Fortunately for the country at this time the Inter-Party Government had a Minister for Finance in Gerard Sweetman, who thought along the same lines as Lemass, regarding the need to form an economic plan in order to take advantage of economic expansion on post-war Europe. To help him along these lines Sweetman plucked out T.K. Whittiger, an aspiring Civil Servant with an Economics degree, and made him Secretary of the Department, which is the number one job in the Civil Service. He had impressed Sweetman with two papers which he had written – one on Economic Development for the Commission on Capital Investment and the other on Capital Investment proposals for the Statistical and Social Society. However, 1955 was an extremely bad year for the Inter-Party Government as the Balance of Payments deficit had gone up from £5.5 million in 1954 to £35.6 million. To counteract this, the Minister for Finance introduced new taxes on consumer spending and levies on a large quantity of imported goods. Economic growth came to a standstill, unemployment rose rapidly and emigration, in the shape of thousands of people leaving the country by the week, followed., Sweetman did not have the backing of his leader, the Cabinet or the Trade Unions. In 1956 Sweetman introduced the new National Development Plan, with the main emphasis being in the use of foreign capital. With this in mind, William Norton, Tánaiste and Minister for Industry & Commerce, embarked on tours of the U.S.A. and Europe to invite and attract foreign investment from these countries. One such success was the attraction and establishment of a £12 million oil refinery in Cork. Though Taoiseach John A. Costello was at pains to point out that he was only inviting in companies whose products were not produced in Ireland and were mostly for export, he came up against De Valera's opposition – "That he must keep Ireland for the Irish", and Boland's' warning that foreign investment would be a danger to our independence. Lemass's objections, using Nationalistic jargon were more on the basis of keeping the party together in opposition.

While in opposition, Lemass was again the main force in reorganising the party. With the influx of young blood or 'Young Turks' by his side, of Charles Haughey, Brian Lenihan, Kevin Boland and Eoin Ryan, he again criss-crossed the length and breadth of the country to revive a party that had gone stale. With the introduction of new and younger recruits, his establishment of Comh-Chomairle and Cáirde Fáil were a promotion to attract new people to the party by stimulating debate on Economic Strategy. The Cleary's Ballroom economic speech was part of his Comh-Chomairle plan.

On the withdrawal of Clann n Poblachta in February 1957, the Inter-Party Government fell. The General Election saw Fianna Fáil return to power with 78 seats – their greatest number yet. The new Cabinet saw the introduction of Jack Lynch, Neil Blaney, Kevin Boland and Michael Moran. Lemass was again in Industry & Commerce but his appointment as Chairman of the Economic Cabinet gave him complete control of economic policy, which touched on every Department, and he was "effectively . . . Taoiseach from then onwards". In 1957, T.K. Whittiger produced his Economic Development Plan. This was approved by the Government in December and the final study was presented to the Dáil in May 1958. This was to become the foundation of the Government's first Programme for Economic Expansion. This programme, announced at the 1956 Ard Fheis was the bones of Government contributions to expenditure in the period 1959-1963. The main provisions of the plan were: -

(1) A higher percentage of Public Capital Expenditure to be spent on productive projects.
(2) Savings to be encouraged.
(3) Direct taxation to be reduced.
(4) The objectives of the plan in each main economic sector were established and the means of achieving them.
(5) Protection to be given to new industries and then only to those who would be able to survive without protection for a short period.
(6) Expansion of export market rather than home market.
(7) Foreign investment and participation in Irish industry to be encouraged.
(8) A growth rate of 2% per annum.

Lemass had changed his old thinking on protection.

The Fianna Fáil ministers in De Valera's last government, 1957
Seated (l. to r.): Oscar Traynor, Frank Aiken, Seán Lemass, Éamon de Valéra, Seán McEntee, Jim Ryan, Paddy Smith.
Standing (l. to r.): Seán Moylan, Kevin Boland, Jack Lynch, Erskine Childers, Neil Blaney, Micheál Ó Móráin.

Lemass becomes Taoiseach

With the Presidential election looming in 1959 and De Valera now unfit to run a new modern economic state, Seán McEntee and Dr Jim Ryan, following a secret meeting of cabinet ministers, approached De Valera and informed him that the consensus of the meeting was that he should run for president. De Valera agreed. On June 3rd 1959, Lemass became Taoiseach on a vote of 75 to 51 and on the 25th of June, De Valera was installed as President having defeated General Seán MacEoin by 120,000 votes. A Referendum on a single vote versus proportional representation on the same day as the presidential election proposed by Fianna Fáil was defeated by over 33,000 votes.

The Taoiseach Seán Lemass in his office, 1965. (Private collection).

Lemass was not slow to take the reins and make known his objectives for his administration. He stated that the task was "to seek the economic foundation of independence". Patriotism would ensure that the love of country meant greater economic endeavour.

On the Northern problem, he stated at his first press conference that the attitude of anti-partition would be changed to "the restoration of the national territory by goodwill rather than force". In an interview with the *Belfast Telegraph* he said that "better relations can be fostered by political co-operation for the mutual benefit" in economic matters and how "policy might be directed as to ensure economic progress in both parts of the country will be impeded as little as possible by . . . political division."

At the Oxford Union debate in October he talked of the two parts of the country coming to an arrangement in which the different culture, religion and education of northern Protestants would be protected. He furthermore re-introduced the concept of reunification under a federal system. In Tralee in July of 1963, he further suggested the federal solution, whereby the Northern Parliament would be allowed to continue with its existing powers under an all-Ireland constitution; in addition, he stated that "the solution of the problem is to be found in Ireland by Irishmen" and . . . as we move towards it, we can be sure that there is no power . . . which can prevent its implementation, when the barriers of suspicion . . . have been whittled away." The old inalienable right of a United Ireland held by the south was now accepting that Northern Protestants had rights too.

This new attitude created the climate for the Northern Premier, Captain Terence O'Neill to invite the Taoiseach to the historic visit to Stormont in 1965. The arrangement was make by TK Whittier and Jim Malley, O'Neill's private secretary. Whittiger had become a close friend of O'Neill and Malley during their numerous encounters at World Bank meetings. For security reasons there was no advance publicity and Lemass confided only in a select few ministerial colleagues. From this famous meeting it was agreed that O'Neill would visit Dublin and that co-operation should be sought in a number of areas with meetings continuing at ministerial level.

On February 9th, O'Neill visited Dublin. There was general satisfaction on both sides of these historic meetings, but of course they would not be complete without the usual adverse reactions from extremists on both sides. There was a significant breakthrough in what was up to then a sort of cold war in North/South relations and was a major achievement, considering the history of the two peoples since 1920. However great this progress was, it still was only in the minor league when compared with Lemass' in his Economic process in the south.   The First Program for Economic Expansion was highly successful and was a major step in transforming a 19th century Agricultural Economy towards a 20th century state. Garrett Fitzgerald stated in *"Studies"* (Winter 1964) that

> *"During this period, the outlook of the people had changed ...from one of cynicism and near despair to one of confidence and self-assurance. The psychological breakthrough is . . . of greater importance . . . in economic achievements, the obstacles to economic and social progress s have always been psychological rather than physical . . ."*

The target set for the economic growth of the programme (1959-1963) was 2% per annum. In fact, it achieved 4.5% per annum against a previous growth rate of 1% from 1949 to 1957. The second programme for economic expansion was not as successful as the first. Though it was drawn up in more detail, setting targets in all sectors of the economy, including targets within each sector, with an overall target rate of 4% the growth rate achieved slowed to 2.5%. Other problems were that the targets were set too high and wage inflation had crept in.

The psychological breakthrough, however, had been made both in the economy and the Northern question and there two achievements should be enough to satisfy anyone, but more was to come. Lemass played a significant part in the Anglo-Irish trade agreement in December 1965 when he achieved a target of a freeing of trade for a 10-year period, as well as more success for Irish agriculture into the British market. This agreement came into effect on January 1st 1966. The Lemass of protectionism of the 30s had now achieved economic progress for the economy; so that the country was now ready for free trade in the 60s. Of course the two programmes for Economic expansion and the Anglo-Irish Agreement were all important steps towards Ireland's entry to the EEC of which Ireland's failure to achieve in the 60s was Lemass' only regret. However it is still doubtful if it would have been possible, given that Britain, on who we were still very dependant export-wise, did not enter either.

A number of problems raised their head in the 1963-64 periods which could have scuttled any minority government, but Lemass was able to sail through with his leadership style. The 1963 budget saw Dr Jim Ryan, Minister for Finance, introduced a turn-over tax of 2.5%. This was a new consumer tax and brought strong opposition from Fine Gael and Labour. Lemass defended it vehemently by stating that if the country wanted economic and social progress, it required higher social spending, which, no doubt, needed higher taxes. It pointed out that the "Fianna Fáil approach is positive, constructive and national" against Fine Gael's, which was "negative, defamatory . . . and political." The loss of a bye-election and three no-confidence motions failed to rattle the minority government. The winning of two bye-elections (Cork city and Kildare) was a turning point as Lemass had stated that the loss of these would be taken as a vote of no confidence and would have precipitated by a general election. The 9th wage round granting a 12% increase in the middle of the bye-election campaigns was no doubt a help in achieving these victories.

A general election did occur however in May 1965. A strong campaign was fought by the opposition in the form of Declan Costello's "Just Society". This document was critical of the government's emphasis on economic policy, stating that it was short on a social policy. Up to now there was little Fine Gael could do as both Sweetman's and Cosgrave's ideas on the economy were similar to Lemass's. Lemass countered the "Just Society" by accepting that a social program was desirable as well as an economic one. The result of the election saw Fianna Fáil increase their number of seats by two and their share of the vote by 3.6%.

In his period in office, Lemass had taken the major issues outside the political sphere and placed them in the hands of his departmental civil servants, the principle of which was T.K. Whittiger. As well as that, he changed his own party by subtly removing the old traditions of patriotic visions to the new practicalities of economic and social progress. To achieve this, he had introduced the young personnel of Haughey, O'Malley, Lenihen and Colley. His retirement in 1966, though a shock to the nation, was another example of his practicality, as he believed it was time for new younger blood to carry on from the excellent base he had achieved for a new Ireland, ready to enter the EEC. He had achieved all this with a minority government.

Jack Lynch

Jack Lynch was born John Mary Lynch in Shandon in the city of Cork on the 15th August 1917, which makes him the first Irish leader who does not have to explain where he was in 1916. He was the fourth son in s family of four boys and two younger sisters. His father Dan, one of three boys, left a small farm in Bantry to work in Cash's in Cork city. His mother, Nora O'Donoghue, who came from a family if seven girls and two sons on a small farm in Plantain, came to Cork to work as a seamstress. She met Dan Lynch in the city and they were married in 1908. The death of his mother, while in his early teens, had a deep effect on Jack, together with the fact that he along with his father three brothers and two sisters, had to move home to share a

Taoiseach Jack Lynch signing Ireland into the EEC.

house with his Aunt Statia's family of eight at 22, Redemption Road. In 1923, Jack started school at St Vincent's Convent and in 1925 he went to the Primary section of the famous North Monastery, where between Primary and Secondary he was to spend the next eleven years. Being a handy hurler and footballer, it did not take long for him to distinguish himself in the Cork and Munster Colleges Competitions. It was not too long before he joined Glen Rovers club and at sixteen was captain of the minor team. He was on the Cork senior hurling team, while still in fifth year at school. In the period 1941 -1946 he won six all-Irelands in a row, five in hurling and one in football, an achievement never since emulated and one that look like it will never again be equalled.

He got his Leaving Certificate in 1936, he joined the Dublin Milk Board, helped no doubt by the fact that he was introduced to its manager, Seán O'Braonáin, who was also recruiting hurlers for the Civil Service GAA club. By Christmas of that year, however, he had returned to Cork as Acting County Register, a position he held for the next seven years. During this time he began his studies for a barrister at University College Cork. As the last two years of his studies had to take place in King's Inn in Dublin, he returned to the capital in an internal Civil Service transfer to the district court clerk's branch, near Leinster House. His transfer was again helped by Paddy O'Ceallaigh, a principal officer in the department of finance and chairman of the Civil Service Football Club, with whom Jack won a Dublin County championship in 1944.

Jack's next move was to be appointed private secretary to the Secretary at the Department of Justice. He was called to the bar in 1945. In 1943, he had met his wife to be, Máirín O'Connor, while on holidays in Glengarrif and they were married on August 10th 1946. Having been called to the bar, he resigned from the civil service and returned to Cork to practice as a barrister. The call to politics came from the Delaney Brothers Cumann before a bye-election in 1946. Jack, however, refused to go at that stage as he would be taking on "Pa" McGrath, who was a long time dedicated member of the party and a friend of Lynch's. He did however leave the door open, and the call came in 1948 general election, again from the Brothers Delaney Cumann and from Tim Crofts, Chairman of the Comhairle Ceanntar, as well as an invite from the Clann na Poblachta party to stand for them. He went forward this time and was duly elected. This was to be the first of eight general elections, which brought Jack Lynch to the highest Parliamentary honours, when he became Taoiseach in 1966. In 1951, he became parliamentary secretary to the government with responsibilities for the Gaeltacht and the congested districts. In this department, he was head of an Inter-Department Committee dealing with conditions in the Gaeltacht and congested districts in which one of his most notable achievements was initiating the special road schemes for the Gaeltacht.

1954 saw Fianna Fáil out of power and Jack Lynch returned to Cork to his Law practice, which flourished and he found it very hard to leave it when the party returned to power in 1957 and the call came from De Valera to join the cabinet. He now became Minister for Education and looked after the Gaeltacht portfolio until Michael O'Morain was appointed Minister for the Gaeltacht nine months later. Though he was education minister for only two years he made significant progress. He abolished the cuts implemented by the previous coalition government in secondary and vocational grants. He removed the marriage ban on women teachers. His emphasis on the spoken Irish prompted him to introduce an oral Irish test in the Leaving Certificate offering bonus marks for it. He set up a commission to examine university accommodation and grants, the result of which was an increase in grants. With regard to Capital Expenditure on Education he began a major building project for the Training College in Drumcondra, doubled the rate of secondary school buildings and initiated the move of University College Dublin to Belfield. The progress in this department was aided no doubt by the fact of De Valera's keen interest in education, a portfolio he himself had held for a few months in a previous government. Jack Lynch was in cabinet when Jim Ryan, then Minister for Finance, introduced Ken Whittiger's first Programme for Economic Expansion and was part of the team that implemented it.

Lynch reaches the top

In 1959 there was a presidential election and De Valera became the country's second president. Seán Lemass was elected Taoiseach. Lemass, sitting at his old desk in his old office in Industry and Commerce, summoned Jack Lynch into the office and said to him, "I want you to sit at this desk". Jack Lynch duly accepted and became Minister for Industry and Commerce together with the portfolio for Transport and Power, a ministry he was to hold for the next six years. During the period, he was to oversee an increase in Free Trade and the introduction to Ireland of investment by overseas companies. During this period, Ireland made its first application for entry to the EEC, but with the UK's application being vetoed by De Gaulle, Ireland decided that it would be unwise to go it alone. In order to prepare itself for Free Trade down the road, and also to eliminate the unfair trading situation that existed between Ireland and the UK on agricultural produce negotiations were opened with the UK government in 1964. This led to the Anglo-Irish Free Trade agreement of 1965. During this period also, a lot of Lynch's time was taken up with strikes which cost Lynch not a few holiday deposits as he was called back from holidays on a number of occasions to settle disputes. In 1964, Paddy Smith resigned as Minister of Agriculture as he felt Lemass was concentrating too much on industry to the detriment of agriculture.

Jack Lynch's next move up the ladder was to Minister of Finance in 1965 and this spurred the feeling that he was being groomed for the top. Lynch, as ever the humble man, dismissed this rumour out of hand. When, in 1966, Lemass suddenly decided to call it a day, he approached Lynch to take over from him and he declined. Weeks later, he, Charlie Haughey and George Colley were called into Lemass's office where discussions took place on his successor. Again, Lynch reminded Lemass of their previous discussions on this subject and his answer at that time. Haughey and Colley indicated that they were interested. When Neil Blayney threw his hat into the ring, the old backbenchers, fearing a split in the party, went to Lemass to press the case for Lynch. Lemass again called Lynch into his office and advised him of the feelings of the backbenchers and that the other candidates were willing to back down if he went forward. He also told Lynch that he had a duty to serve the party, even as leader. Having had a long discussion with his wife, Lynch decided to go forward. On Lemass's retirement, the other candidates, with the exception of Colley, backed down. Lynch won the vote handsomely by 52 votes to 19. Later, he was elected Taoiseach in the Dáil by 71 votes to Liam Cosgrave's 64. In the next few years, things seemed to go smoothly enough for Lynch as Taoiseach. His main tasks were concentrated in turning his mind to Europe, handling an outbreak of foot and mouth disease and an attempt to change the electoral system. Having got on a winning streak with wins in bye-elections in South Kerry and Waterford, he lost the referendum to give the country a single vote system and received another setback in Europe as De Gaulle vetoed the UK. In 1968, one of the key actions that was to play a significant part in our growth and development, was the introduction of free secondary education by

Jack Lynch receives his seal of office as Taoiseach from President Éamon de Valera in 1966.

Donagh O'Malley, Minister for Education. His untimely death a year later deprived the country of a man of vision, whose policy on education was way ahead of his contemporaries.

Shortly after becoming Taoiseach, Jack Lynch travelled, as his predecessor did, to meet Captain Terence O'Neill, where he received a cold welcome from Rev Ian Paisley, who snowballed his car. Jack Lynch's policy for the North was unity by agreement. Fianna Fáil's policy had always been unity by peaceful means and Lynch said he could see no difference between these two aims. Following this meeting with O'Neill, Lynch as a gesture of goodwill was willing to offer a 10% preference to genuine Northern Ireland Manufacturing firms, exporting to the South over and above that provided in the Anglo-Irish Free Trade Area agreement.

Troubles in the North

It is generally accepted that the civil rights march in Derry on October 5th 1968 was the beginning of what became the start of the 'troubles'. A speech by Northern Premier, Capt Terrence O'Neill on television on December 9th which seemed to give hope for the future was short-lived when a loyalist mob ambushed a peaceful Peoples' Democracy march at Burntullet in early January 1969. This was followed in mid-January by the resignation of Deputy Premier Brian Faulkner and a request of a number of deputies for O'Neill's resignation. O'Neill called a general election for February 24th but the result was humiliating for O'Neill. By February 1969, the British government were aware of the seriousness and the uncertain outlook for the North and following a meeting of Wilson (Prime minister), Callaghan (Home Secretary) and Healy (Defence) the following Modus Operandi was produced. Callaghan had already produced a draft Bill for Direct Rule. And Healy initiated contingency plans for military assistance in the case of the following scale of developments: - (a) Sporadic civil disturbances, (b) More serious but isolated rioting (c) Widespread urban rioting (d) Widespread collapse of law and order (e) a situation where the Northern Government would refuse to be taken over by Westminster. By August sectarian conflict was rife.

A peaceful march, demanding civil rights for the Catholic nationalist population in North by the North of Ireland Civil Rights Association (NICRA) ended up with a siege of Derry by the police and 'B' Specials. Fear of a catholic massacre in Derry necessitated a cabinet meeting in Dublin. Blaney, Boland and Haughey advocated sending in the troops from the south to protect the Catholics in Derry and by creating an international incidence, would, as it were, require the intervention of an Independent United Nations peace force. Recent Government papers released indicate that the Dublin government did contemplate incursions by the southern army to relieve the catholic population of Derry in a Doomsday situation. This was a testing one for Fianna Fail as it brought to the surface different interpretations of reunification and indeed, republicanism within the party. There was no precedence for this since the formation of the party. As well as that, this was the first time that violence, particularly as it was happening in the Bogside and the Falls, was brought into the homes of the south by the medium of television. Together with that as the reunification of the country was the No. 1 aim of the Fianna Fáil party it was only reasonable that the minority in the North would look south for help as Fianna Fáil were in government. There were some who felt that the party for too long were paying lip service to reunification and saw this as an opportunity to put it to the test once and for all. Three were some, no doubt who saw it as a political opportunity to further their prominence within the party. Then there was Jack Lynch, and a considerable number of the party, as it turned out, who favoured a more restrained political approach. They felt that an invasion by southern troops would cause immediate reaction from northern Protestants, endangering the lives of many of the Catholic population in Belfast and other isolated areas. It would furthermore involve the south in a confrontation, with the added danger of the loss of Foreign Investment and the resultant adverse affects on the economy. A compromise was eventually reached whereby immediate talks would be demanded with the UK regarding the constitutional position of the northern counties, Field hospitals to be arranged immediately along the border to facilitate Catholics injured and a call to the United Nations to install a peacekeeping force. All this was to be publicly announced on television by the Taoiseach. This was the famous broadcast that has since posted the question of whether Jack Lynch was to say "will not stand by . . ." or "will not stand idly by". The bones of the speech was that "The Irish Government can no longer stand [idly] by and see innocent people injured . . . It is obvious that the RUC is no longer accepted as an impartial force. Neither would . . . British Soldiers be acceptable nor . . be likely to restore peaceful ambitions . . . in the long term . . ."

The cabinet meeting the next morning decided on the following points:

(a)   That the Minister of External Affairs would seen an immediate meeting with the Foreign Secretary or Jim Callaghan,

(b)   That he should seek the support of all ambassadors in Dublin re. appeal to the UN.

(c)   That a similar approach should be made to member states where Ireland had not got representations. Though it was felt that the approach to the Security Council members, where the UK had a representative, would fail, it was felt that a high-profile attempt be seen to be made.

(d)   The provision of troops at the border to protect the field hospitals

(e)   Expand Garda intelligence in the north

(f)   Set up a committee comprising the secretaries of the Departments of Justice, External Affairs, Defence and Local Government (it excluded the secretary of finance), to keep the situation continuous review and to advise the Taoiseach

(g)   That as sum of money - amount and the channel of disbursement of which be determined by the Minster of Finance should be made available from the Exchequer to provide aid for the victims of the current unrest in the six counties.

Recent government papers in the UK show that if Government pressure on Northern premier, Captain Terrence O'Neill, to speed up reforms were pushed too much, he would have to resign. This turned out to be a self-fulfilling prophesy as the party refused to row in behind him and he resigned on April 28th. The British government were also studying other options on areas like whether it would be better to send in the troops or a UDI. Sending in the troops might look as if they were favouring the Unionists whereas the UDI would not be politically, geographically, economically or militarily sound as well as it would possibly put pressure on the Dublin Government to reclaim the fourth "green field". In the case of the UDI, also, the new administration might be too stringent and not capable of a fair law and order system and the Britain's would have to re-intervene. At the end of the day, with James Chichester-Clark installed as the new premier, the UK Government maintained the same policy until Mid-August with O'Neill's successor, of Stormont solving its own problems of reform. The UK would only intervene with troops in the direst of emergencies and only then at the behest of the Northern Government. If troops were necessary it would have to be in line with UK policy and any escalation of events requiring extra troops would be in the knowledge that they were both aware of the implications. A call by Lynch requiring a meeting with Wilson was rejected. The excuse given by the British Ambassador to Lynch was that it might undermine the new Northern Premier.

In mid-July, rioting broke out again and at the end of the month, Callaghan told the cabinet that the fears that John Hume had vis a vis the upcoming Apprentice Boys March on August 12th and that if it resulted in rioting and the RUC could not handle it, the troops might be needed. At this meeting, Wilson, Callaghan and Healy got the authority to handle whatever came up before the next cabinet meeting. A request by Paddy Hillery, Minister for External Affairs to ban the march was rebuffed by Michael Steward, Home Office, stating that it would be easier to control it than ban it and telling Hillery that it was a UK internal affair anyhow. Hillery warned that if there was violence he would have to advise the UN security council. On 6th August, Chichester-Clark was furious at Callaghan's comment that if troops were to be deployed, Stormont would be temporarily suspended as the UK could not be responsible for actions that troops might take under the Stormont regime. In a meeting with Callaghan and Robert Porter, Home Office, on august 8th, Chichester-Clark informed them that any amendment to the Ireland Act of 1920 or suspension of Stormont would bring a strong, even violent reaction from Protestants. When the troops were eventually deployed on the eve of the Apprentice Boys march, Callaghan asked Wilson if it would be necessary to appoint a Minister for Northern Affairs and Wilson said no, as it might precipitate the resignation of Chichester-Clark.

The amazing thing in Dublin at this time was that in eleven Cabinet meetings of the new Government between July 3rd and August 7th, no mention was made of Northern Ireland. The first meeting concerning the 'troubles' in the North was an emergency meeting on 13th August. The only other meeting that there are minutes for was on September 9th, at which it was decided that the Minister of External Affairs would bring the situation to the General Assembly of the United Nations.

At the same time as Fianna Fáil were going through a soul-searching mission, a similar situation was happening in the IRA. As the 1956-1962 armed campaign had ended in disaster, senior members within the organisation were looking at new strategies. As most of the policies up to now were aimed at the North with a view to influencing the people down south, it was now felt that attention should be turned towards the Government in Dublin, who the IRA felt had become snug and were concentrating on a Capitalist/Catholic ideology. Chief amongst these was Cathal Goulding, who felt that the IRA needed a wider and clearer left-wing policy to take on the Fianna Fáil Government. The belief was that war had failed because there were no clear political objectives and there was a need for a political and economic strategy. On the other side, Seán MacStiophán while agreeing to a certain degree with the fact that a social policy was needed, did not however want to abandon the war strategy. From their headquarters in Gardiner Street in Dublin, Goulding, with the aid of Peadar O'Donnell, George Gilmore, Dr. Roy Johnson and Anthony Loughlin, started to put together the new strategy. They felt that by infiltrating the Trade Unions and aligning with other left-wing bodies they would take on the business classes with its TACA dinners and the like. Funnily, they also decided to become involved in protecting Georgian Dublin from the modern office blocks that the Government were creating with their Economic Plan. The beginning of the real split in the IRA would seem to have its origins in Goulding's attempt to seek the abandonment of the Abstentionist policy, which went to the very core of I.R.A.'s policy at the IRA Convention in 1964. Ruairí O'Brádaigh and Seán MacStiophán were against the motion and it was rejected. Other policies on economic and social agitation and cooperation with left-wing organisations were adopted. Though O'Brádaigh and MacStiophán went along with this for the moment they still did not want the IRA to neglect Military preparedness. Goulding did not agree with this strategy.

The Northern units were completely disillusioned with this and many had drifted away from the organisation, so when the troubles broke out in the North in 1969 the organisation was rife for a split. Goulding, Dr. Johnson and a Northern Catholic lawyer, Kevin Agnew, at a Wolfe Tone Society meeting in 1966 had attempted to influence the members by convincing them that sectarianism was created by U.K. interests, and that by infiltrating the Trades Unions it would be possible to convince the Protestant working class and thus bringing them over on our side would create the conditions for unity. The meeting did not go along with this but instead agreed on a Civil Rights Campaign. This was really the beginning of the Civil Rights Movement in the North. Though the real motivation of the movement was civil rights, Paisley and his followers painted the campaign as a way that the IRA would use to restart the armed campaign. On the contrary, Goulding's motivation for being involved with NICRA was to show the ability of both the Dublin and Stormont Governments to bring about reforms for the working class. However, once the campaign was set in train, it was perceived by Unionists as another attempt at a Nationalist military campaign, with the ensuing Loyalist backlash. This was to eventually put it beyond the control of Goulding and company. On October 5th, Eamonn McCann headed the first march of the Northern Ireland Civil Rights Association and this brought about the expected reaction from the R.U.C. In fact, there was even a more vicious reaction than was expected.

When Jack Lynch became Taoiseach in 1966, it was thought by many, especially the chief pretenders for the position, (Colley, Haughey and Blaney), that he was a caretaker Taoiseach. So here in 1969 is a Taoiseach who has won an election with an overall majority for the first time since 1957 and had no signs of retiring. Sabres had begun to rattle after the election when Lynch, in forming his Cabinet, had been unable to move Blaney from Agriculture. Blaney had established a strong position in the party as an excellent organiser, especially for winning bye-elections. He also was unable to remove Boland from Local Government. Colley, it is believed, was having a swipe at Haughey's anticipated ambitions for the top with comment at an Ógra Fianna Fáil conference dinner speech in Galway in May 1967 that, "Some people in high places appear to have low standards". Haughey, with his own spin doctor Tony Grey of the *Irish Times* and admirer John Healy, 'Backbencher' in the *Irish Times,* was getting great press as a rising star. As the number one aim of the part was the re-unification of the country and since Fianna Fáil had the mantle of being the trusted guardians of that policy, when the troubles broke out in the North it was a testing time for this policy as well as a chance for a tilt at the top job by the pretenders. Since Jack Lynch's background was not steeped in Fianna Fáil tradition and as he was looked on by some people in the party especially Haughey, Blaney and Boland as not having a republican ethos, this was a chance for a change at the helm. It was also the first major chance since 1923 that the opportunity arose for Fianna Fáil's re-unification policy to be tested, and positive results, by not alone that element of the party, but by a large section of the population, would have brought elevation for these people within the party and even immortality, no doubt..

Other aspects at the time which seem to contribute to the events of the day were the pressures by Blaney and Boland on Lynch to introduce the single vote electoral system to copper-fasten Fianna Fáil's advantage in General Elections, whereas the Northern Ireland Civil Rights Association were trying to break the stranglehold the Unionists had in the North by attempting to change from the single vote system to the proportional representation system which one had in the South. Northern politicians speaking against the Unionist's monopoly in the North due to the single vote system issued a warning to the people of the South against the system. A previous attempt in 1959 to introduce the single vote in the South was defeated, though De Valera was elected President on the same day. The result was even more convincing on this occasion as the people voted 60/40 against it in the country and 70/30 in the urban areas. In the election of 1969, Haughey, Director of Elections, Blaney and Boland played a significant part in obtaining 75 of the 144 seats, part of which was a 'reds under the bed' campaign which killed off Labour's socialist policy and was also, no doubt, a shot at Cathal Goulding's left-wing politics as well.

Peter Berry, Secretary of the Department of Justice at the time, was to play a significant part in the activities which would later lead to what became known as the Arms Trial in May 1970. on August 20th, 1969. He reported to the Government that there had been a meeting between a Government Minister and Cathal Goulding, then Chief of Staff of the IRA. Haughey admitted that it might be himself as he was asked to meet someone and it turned out to be Goulding. This was accepted, as it was well known of Haughey's anti-IRA stance when he was Minister for Justice in 1961. Later still, there were rumours that Haughey had promised £50,000 to Goulding and that his brother Padraig (Jock) Haughey, along with John Kelly, a Belfast IRA member, were attempting to buy arms for the North in London. Jock Haughey and Kelly were negotiating to buy arms with a British Intelligence agent, a Captain Randall, who was later exposed when he tried to recruit a republican as an agent and was saved from certain execution by Captain James Kelly, who himself was to become a leading light in the Arms Trial. He, along with journalist Seamus Brady, were to become the intelligence agents for the Government's sub-committee in the North.

Early in October a meeting of about fifteen to twenty republicans which was reputed to include Cathal Goulding met with Captain Kelly at the Bailieboro Hotel, owned by Captain Kelly's brother. The expenses for the meeting, about £500, came from the Sub-Committee's Relief Fund and it was discussed at the meeting that about £50,000 was available to purchase arms. Peter Berry learned of this meeting and he contacted Haughey and advised him of the goings on in Bailieboro. Haughey listened to what he had to say but did not take action. Later on, when Berry found out about Haughey's involvement in the Bailieboro meeting, he contacted the Taoiseach. On October 18th Jack Lynch visited Berry in hospital, where he was undergoing tests, and Berry informed him of the Bailieboro meeting which had IRA members present, of Capt. Kelly's promises of £50,000 for arms and that a lot of money was spent on drinks. Though Lynch told Jim Gibbons about Berry's report and Gibbons maintained he advised Lynch in October of Ministers meeting undesirable republicans, Lynch not alone took no action at the time, but stated that he knew nothing of these events until April 20th, 1970.

There is no doubt that at the time a very serious situation prevailed in the North and Martin Mansergh adequately described it in a critique of Justine O'Brien's book *The Arms Trial*, when he stated that this book failed "to convey the white heat of the civil rights protest as the old Stormont began to collapse". Mansergh shows "that pressures on Dublin to protect communities form rampaging loyalist mobs and bigoted security forces were huge". One must also remember that we were seeing this on television in the South at first hand for the first time. The Lemass/Lynch policy at the time was not, or was not seen to be, adequate to protect the minority in the North. The cabinet realised contingency plans were necessary and the extent of these plans seem to be the differences that were perceived by different factions within the Government and higher echelons of the army at that time. In Vincent Brown's articles on the Arms Trial in his *Magill* of May, June and July of 1981, he quotes a copy of a formal Government directive issued to the Irish Army Chief of Staff by Jim Gibbons, Minister of Defence in February 1970:- "The Government have instructed me to convey to the army a directive that plans be immediately put in train for operating in Northern Ireland, in the event the situation (in the opinion of the Government) warrants interference. The Government further directs that training and planning programmes be directed to cater for such an emergency". This directive was later formally translated into still more explicit terms: - "The Government directs that the army (1) prepare to train the forces for incursions into Northern Ireland, (2) make weapons and ammunition available and (3) make gas masks available". It would seem therefore according to the article "that the provision of arms for distribution in Northern Ireland, when the Government warranted it, was Government policy". This would also suggest that the Taoiseach knew more than he admitted later. The fact that he did not act at that time may have a lot to do with the fact that he was a compromise leader, felt unsure of himself due, on the one hand to his lack of stature compared with his predecessors, plus the fact that he was surrounded by Ministers like Blaney and Boland who were strong in the republican aims of the party. It would demonstrate that Lynch had no real control of the Cabinet at that time and didn't not have so until after Cosgrove informed him about he aborted guns episode in April 1970, in which case he had no option but to sack Haughey and Blaney and with the resultant resignation of Boland and the backing of the rest of the Cabinet, Jack Lynch suddenly realised his strength. There is also the other opinion that he was waiting for more concrete evidence to nail Haughey and Blaney. Whichever it was he definitely established himself as the boss until late 1979.

With the arrival of the British army, the immediate time-bomb in 1969 was averted. Behind the scenes however, events continued which eventually led to the Arms Trial in May 1970. Although many weapons made their way over the border in the late stages of 1969, these were mainly coming from private sources. There was a situation where guns coming from the South were brought into the car part in Dáil Éireann and switched into another car and taken North.

An attempt was made to send weapons to the North in April 1970 when things were getting out of hand in the Ballymurphy area during an Orange Parade which had been sanctioned by the Government and had the full support of the Army. Blaney got the Gardaí to intercept Defence Minister Gibbons at Naas on his way home to Kilkenny to inform him that the Nationalists there were about to be murdered. Gibbons, unable to contact the Taoiseach, who was on holidays in Cork, ordered 500 army weapons to be transferred to abase in Dundalk. When Lynch eventually found out about the transfer of the arms, he ordered them to be returned. This was the only action he took at the time.

The Arms Trial

The attempt to import arms began when Captain Kelly flew to Hamburg where he met Otto Schleuter, an arms dealer who was introduced to him by Albert Luykx, a Belgian businessman living in Ireland. The arms were to be shipped on *City of Dublin* into Dublin, and Capt. Kelly and John Kelly, Belfast IRA, were there to meet it. Due to the lack of proper clearance papers at Antwerp the guns did not arrive. An attempt to import the arms by air from Vienna in a scheduled Aer Lingus flight came unstuck, as transport of firearms was prohibited by international regulations. Then negotiations opened with Aer Turas, a subsidiary of Aer Lingus, but this also failed to materialise due to the lack of an end-user's certificate, which Capt. Kelly seemed to be completely ignorant of. Because of suspicion arising out of this, John Squires, Aer Turas, became suspicious and rang the Department of Transport and Power who then rang Peter Berry in the Department of Justice. At the same time Special Branch were informing the Justice Department of a conspiracy to import arms. On top of all this a customs officer, talking to Capt. Kelly at the airport became suspicious when he saw the large presence of Special Branch at the airport, and he rang Anthony Fagan in Finance. He in turn rang Haughey and Colonel Hefferon, advising them that unless somebody rang Chief Superintendent Fleming the cargo would be seized. Haughey decided that the consignment, "whatever it was", should be called off. Fagan instructed Capt. Kelly to abort the operation. Even though the importation of arms never materialised, the fact that 'the dogs in the street' knew about it, the course of Justice now took over. Whether Jack Lynch was aware of the operation from his first meeting in October 1969 with Peter Berry, or his subsequent meetings on April 13th and April 20th, 1970, he hesitated to take any action. Peter Berry, being totally frustrated at this time by Lynch not taking any action, went to President De Valera and asked him to request Jack Lynch to prevent an operation which he believed to be a major threat to the State. The President told Berry it was his duty to report it to the Taoiseach. When Berry reported to Lynch that he had gone to the President he was furious. At the same time, the Minister for Justice, Micheál Ó Moráin was becoming an embarrassment to the Government, from the fact that it was alleged he was no longer capable of doing his job due to his drinking bouts. It came to a crescendo when he collapsed at a Canadian Law function at the Gresham Hotel and a few days later ended up in hospital. April 22nd was Budget Day and the Minister for Finance, Haughey, due to an accident when he fell from his horse while riding, was unable to present the Budget and it was then introduced by Lynch himself. Lynch's excuse for not sacking the two Ministers at this time is that because of Haughey's hospitalisation – he was waiting to sack the two Ministers together.

However, on April 30th he told Berry that the matter was ended. He informed the Cabinet on May 1st that he had challenged the two but they denied any involvement in the affair and that the matter was now ended.

By this time the Special Branch were fed up with the inaction and it is believed that someone high up in the Branch decided to inform Liam Cosgrave, Leader of the Opposition. After a number of unsuccessful attempts to leak it to the newspapers, and meeting with his closest colleagues, Tom O'Higgins, Michael O'Higgins, Mark Clinton, Denis Jones and Jim Dooge, he decided to inform Lynch. On Monday, May 4th, Lynch went to Mount Carmel hospital and asked for the resignation of Michael O'Morain and received it in no uncertain terms. Later in the day, when informing the Dáil of the said resignation, Liam Cosgrave asked Lynch would there be any other resignations, and Lynch replied that he did not know what the Deputy was talking about. After the Dáil meeting Cosgrave went to Lynch and informed him of what he knew. Lynch said it was true, but that Gibbons and Heffron were not involved. At two o'clock the next morning Lynch issued a statement through his P.R. Department that Haughey and Blaney had been fired. Kevin Boland and Paudge Brennan, Parliamentary Secretary, then resigned.

The morning after the sackings the Taoiseach asked for an adjournment of the Dáil for an hour so that he could attend a meeting of the Fianna Fáil parliamentary party to discuss the crisis, much to the displeasure of Liam Cosgrave. At the meeting of the Parliamentary party, Lynch managed to get the support of the Parliamentary party – Blaney and Boland included. Haughey pledged his loyalty in a letter from his hospital bed stating he agreed with his dismissal by the Taoiseach on the grounds "that not even the slightest suspicion should attach to any member of Government". Back in the Dáil at ten o'clock, the Taoiseach stated that his main business was a motion to appoint Des O'Malley as Minister for Justice to replace Michael O'Morain, and that he would debate the arms crisis later in the week. Liam Cosgrave stated that the situation was so grave that the Government should resign. Conor Cruise O'Brien suggested that the matter would have been covered up but for Cosgrave's intervention. Des O'Malley was appointed Minister on a vote of 72 to 65, supported by Blaney and Boland. The Dáil met again at 10.30 the next morning, on Friday, May 8th. The initial business was the appointments of Gerry Collins, Bobby Molly and Gerry Croinin to replace Haughey, Blaney and Boland. This was a record session of the Dáil as it lasted thirty-six and a half hours in which 69 Deputies, sixteen Fianna Fáil, spoke on the arms debacle. The appointments were carried by 73 votes to 66. Lynch, having now established himself in both Government and within the party, handed the question of the attempted importation of arms over to the Attorney General. As a result of this, Charles Haughey, Neil Blaney, Captain Kelly, John Kelly and Albert

Luykx were arrested and were charged with gun-running. In July, Blaney denied all knowledge of the arms importation and as there was no evidence to link him to it, the charge was dismissed in the Circuit Court. Haughey and the others went to trial on September 22nd on the charge of conspiring to illegally import arms. After six days the Judge, Andreas O'Keefe, took exception to an accusation of being biased by Council for Luykx, dismissed the jury and ordered a new trial. The second trial began on October 6th and lasted fourteen days, at the end of which, Haughey was found not guilty on the basis that he did not know that the shipment contained arms. His contention was that the consignment was something "needed by the army to fulfil the [Government] contingency plans" to help the people in the North. The others were also let off on the grounds that they believed that they were working on orders from the highest authority, i.e. with Government approval. One issue that raised its head during the trial was a conflict of evidence between Haughey and witness Jim Gibbons which led the Judge to state that one of them was guilty of perjury, plus the fact that the evidence of the others vis-a-vis Government sanction would be a further conflict of evidence. Haughey, on his acquittal, stated that "those responsible for this debacle have no option but to take the honourable course open to them . . . there is some dissatisfaction about the leadership at the moment. The Taoiseach's position . . . will be decided by the parliamentary party". Lynch however, who was in the U.S.A., dispelled all doubts about who was boss when he returned to Ireland and was met at the airport by a large group of T.D.s, Senators and all the Cabinet, except for two who were abroad. The next day at the parliamentary meeting Haughey's challenge died. To further frustrate Haughey, the opposition put down a vote of no confidence in Jim Gibbons which Lynch turned into a vote of confidence in himself. Haughey had to swallow hard and together with Blaney voted confidence in Lynch and Gibbons, who had had a conflict of evidence with Haughey in the courts only days earlier. Boland could take no more and resigned his seat rather than vote. After this Haughey made no more statements and decided to buy time, whereas Blaney and Boland, more so, disappeared into the political wilderness.

The main questions that come from the arms crisis were: -

(1) Did the Government knowingly or inadvertently authorise the importation of arms?
(2) Was it a sub-plot confined to any combination of the following – Blaney, Haughey, Gibbons, Captain Kelly and Colonel Heffron?
(3) How much of (1) or (2) were involved or responsible for the setting up of the Provisional IRA. Or is this a myth?

To one, one could say that from Government papers released

recently that there was a government policy to make incursions into the North in a doomsday situation. The fact that no minutes were made of a number of Cabinet meetings at the time would lead one to believe that something more than meets the eye was being discussed. Did the Government supply Haughey with the finance and then turn a blind eye to what Haughey, Blaney and company might do with it? It would seem logical that Haughey, Minister for Finance, with a brilliant career as Leader just around the corner beckoning, would jeopardise this with the importation of illegal arms. He may go along with what was happening, either 'not knowing' or 'not wanting to know' what the details were. How much was Jim Gibbons involved?

Recent revelations from both the Irish and British Government papers suggest that he was not as innocent as he or Lynch tried to portray. Valuable parts of Colonel Heffron's statement to the Gardaí which would have implicated Gibbons were deleted before they got to the Book of Evidence. There were sixteen deletions in all. These irregularities were discovered lately by Captain Kelly, who has spent the last thirty years trying to clear his good name. The papers also show that the then new Minister for Justice, Des O'Malley, had seen the original papers and had signed them as having been read. He says today that he cannot recall the papers. Who was responsible for the deletions and what were they trying to hide? It seems obvious that someone was trying to protect Gibbons. As Gibbons could legally import arms as Minister of Defence, then his involvement would have legalised the whole operation and there may have been no reason for the Arms Trial.

Who was protecting Gibbons, and why? Was this a chance to get rid of people like Haughey, Blaney and Boland; the strong republicans within the party? Was somebody trying to appease the British? From British Government papers released recently we learn that secret dispatches from the British Ambassador in Dublin in 1970 record that Lynch had confided in him his exasperation and fury at Gibbons' disastrous testimony and how he might have to get rid of him. Publicly, Lynch was defending Gibbons and even made him Minister for Agriculture. Having dismissed Haughey and Blaney on the basis that even "the slightest suspicion should be attached to a Minister", he gives Gibbons one of the most senior ministries. Captain Kelly and Colonel Heffron would have no reason to doubt the legality of the operation if Gibbons, Blaney and Haughey were seeming to carry out Government policy. As regards the possibility of the Government helping to form the Provisional IRA, this is a myth. The split in the IRA dealt with earlier, had begun a long time before the troubles broke out. The fear that the troubles did invoke in the North brought all of the Northern Nationalists together from old militant IRA to respectable politicians like Paddy Devlin, Paddy O'Hanlon and Paddy Kennedy, to ordinary enlightened citizens. It was these respectable politicians who came south looking for assistance and guns. Haughey, who held the purse strings stated at all times that he needed a group of acceptable people to distribute the money and assistance to their besieged colleagues in the North, and this job had to be done by Northerners. We know that when Captain Kelly visited Gerry Fitt's house at an early stage of the Troubles in Belfast, John Kelly, a well-known IRA activist in Belfast was there. We also know that there was quite a mixture of political factions at the meeting in Bailieboro, so it was quite difficult to distinguish the different allegiances and objectives at that time. It was only natural that some money would have got into the hands of some people who would eventually become the Provisionals, but it is very doubtful that the southern Government or a subsection of it would be instrumental in setting up the Provisionals.

Jack Lynch - Part Two

After the Arms Trial the Public Accounts Committee was set up to investigate where the £100,000 allocated for the relief of the Northern Nationalist was spent. This was, in effect, another trial of Charlie Haughey, who had sole responsibility as to how and where it was spent. Padraig (Jock) Haughey, a brother of Charlie's was called as a witness and refused to answer any question and was sentenced to six months in prison for contempt of court; a sentence that was overturned by the Supreme Court. This judgement, plus restraints by the Official Secrets Act, ensured that the results and conclusions of the Committee came to nought. From now on, all statements on the North were to be the sole responsibility of Jack Lynch, a motion that was seconded by Des O'Malley, who years later left Fianna Fáil to set up the Progressive Democrats as a result of Charlie Haughey's 'Uno Duce' policy of one voice on the North.

By now Jack Lynch had assumed complete control of the party and the Government. In the period 1970-1973, a number of changes were taking place in the party. Martin O'Donoghue, an Economics lecturer at Trinity College, had come in to advise Jack Lynch and became the General Economic Adviser. A young accountant from Galway, Seamus Brennan, replaced the retiring Tommy Mullins as General Secretary of the party. Esmond Smith became Research Director and Frank Dunlop was made Press Officer. In this period Fianna Fáil had engineered an 83% backing in a referendum to join the EEC, with only Labour voting against. Though they managed to hold on in Government until 1973, a number of things were beginning to go against them. Labour, at their convention in Cork had opened the door for coalition with Fine Gael. Cosgrave and Corish knew that they would have to combine to get Fianna Fáil out. Lynch was beginning to isolate himself from the parliamentary party and surround himself with non-elected specialists. He had received a number of setbacks that, as he described in an autobiography in *Magill*, that nearly made up his mind to resign as Taoiseach, but was urged to stay on by his minders. One such incident was the Littlejohn affair. The Littlejohn brothers were extradited from Britain for bank robberies in the Republic. They pleaded that they were working for British Intelligence and that the robberies were a deliberate plan to blame the IRA and force the Government to introduce internment. Documentation from the British Government linking the brothers to British Intelligence had been shown to Jack Lynch but he denied ever seeing the papers. Later however, having been reminded by the opposition, he admitted to seeing the documents, but 'due to a lapse of memory' he had forgotten that he had seen them. The Minister of Justice, Des O'Malley had also seen the papers and knew Lynch had seen them, but chose to remain silent. If one looks at his silence on the deletions to Colonel Heffron's statement in the Book of Evidence in the Arms Trial, it makes one wonder what was covered during that period of time. A broken ankle sustained in a boating accident by Lynch was another incident that prompted him to resign, but his minders again insisted he stayed as he was central to the plans that he lead Fianna Fail into the election. Throughout this time Charlie Haughey was not sitting back doing nothing. He was doing the rounds of the cummain throughout the country, accompanied by P.J. Mara and other close friends. His popularity was growing rapidly attending these 'rubber chicken' functions the length and breadth of the country and he got to know a lot of the new budding deputies who were to be a big part of his backing in 1979 when he unseated Lynch. This strategy worked very well and Haughey's popularity and career began to take off again. In 1972 he was re-elected as one of the five Honorary Vice-presidents of the party at the Ard Fheis of that year.

In the previous November Minister for Justice, Des O'Malley introduced the Offences Against the State Act Bill to the Dáil. This Bill, when it would become law, would consist of non-jury courts for people accused of terrorist acts, who could be charged and convicted of IRA membership on the word of a Chief Superintendent. He had been prevented from introducing Internment without trial by objections from the other Ministers. Though Labour and Fine Gael had planned to vote against the Bill, Fine Gael leader, Liam Cosgrave, was for it, and was in danger of losing his leadership on account of it and other issues. During the debate, two loyalist bombs went off in Dublin killing a number of people and maiming many others, and this caused Fine Gael to row in behind their Leader and the Bill was passed with a huge majority.

In February 1973 Jack Lynch, perceiving that the opposition were in a bit of disarray, decided to call an election. Fine Gael and Labour, though caught by surprise, or probably because of it, came together to fight the election on a fourteen point plan. An objection to the ratification of Charlie Haughey's selection as a candidate by Frank Aiken caused a bit of bother in the Fianna Fáil camp, but interventions by De Valera and Aiken's fellow Louth Deputy, Joe Farrell, resolved the problem and also prevented it from adverse publicity. Jack Lynch was able to announce at a function that Frank Aiken was not contesting the election for health reasons. Though Fianna Fáil were defeated by the combined Fine Gael-Labour Coalition, they in fact increased their share of the vote to 46.%. This was, in essence, a remarkable achievement in view of the trauma and soul-searching that Fianna Fáil had encountered since 1969. Three months after the General Election Erskine Childers defeated Tom O'Higgins, the Fine Gael candidate, to become Ireland's third President. Fine Gael had high hopes that O'Higgins would break the stranglehold

Fianna Fáil had on the Presidency, due to the fact that they were in Government and that O'Higgins had given De Valera a good run in the previous contest.

The main Fianna Fáil deputies making their mark now in opposition were O'Malley, Colley and especially Haughey. Pressure began to build up for a return of Haughey to the front bench, and although Lynch decided to ignore it throughout 1974, he had no alternative in a re-shuffle in 1975 but to do so, even against the strong wishes of Mrs. Childers, now widow of the President, who had died suddenly in office in 1974. Haughey was given the Health portfolio but refused any strings attached by Lynch regarding Northern Ireland policy, as it might seem he was buying himself back. Lynch bought it. Once restored to the Front Bench Haughey did concur with Lynch's policy on the North at the 1975 Ard Fheis, adding 'that Jack Lynch is the only Leader we have'. However, at a later stage Michael O'Kennedy, spokesman on Foreign Affairs, put a new Draft before the party on Northern Policy which was calling for "the ordered withdrawal of the British from the North". Though Jack Lynch was not in favour of this approach, its popularity within the party carried the day. Haughey backed it and this was an initial factor in his reaching the top in 1979. On June 18th, 1973, a meeting was held in the house of Jack Lynch in Rathgar to put forward a platform for the coming General Election. Lynch himself was the only politician present at the meeting, which included such prominent people as Martin O'Donoghue, barrister Hugh O'Flaherty, and IMI lecturer, Noel Mulcahy. There were others present who to this day are not known. This dependence on non-politician specialists, to the exclusion of the parliamentary party, especially the backbenchers, started a process that was to come to a head in 1979 and was one of the main factors that created a situation that unseated Lynch as Taoiseach and replaced him with Charlie Haughey.

The Coalition's policies were soon seen to be not working. Prices, mainly due to the oil crisis were rising; Ritchie Ryan was introducing a supplementary budget which increased the price of petrol by 11p per gallon; the Public Services Bill was getting out of hand; Banks, bidding in both sides, were driving up the price of land; all were leading to a 'hairshirt' economic environment whereby Cosgrave was being portrayed in the light entertainment and cartoon media as 'The Minister for Hardship'. The debacle of Paddy Donegan's blunder as Minister of Defence, in which he called the new President, Cearbhall Ó Dálaigh's referral of the Emergency Powers Act (1796) to the Supreme Court as a "thundering disgrace" causing the President to tender his resignation. No action was taken against Donegan, both of these decisions angered many people. IRA activity was also rampant and came to a head with the murder of the British Ambassador, Christopher Ewart Biggs. Throughout 1976, Fianna Fáil's ratings were going up in the polls, though this was ignored by everybody except staunch Fianna Fáil followers. The strong opposition by Haughey, Collins, O'Malley, Colley and O'Kennedy to the Coalition's Emergency Powers legislation helped to stir the old republican ethos within the party and the republican electorate in general. To counteract all this, James Tully, Minister for Local Government, was attempting a major redrawing of constituencies in an operation that became known as the 'Tullymander', which was meant to keep Fianna Fáil out of power for many years. It was a major manipulation of 3-seaters in Dublin and 4-seaters in the country and, as we will see, it boomeranged back on its inventors.

The fact that the Coalition were also boring the people with their obsession that borrowing had to be reduced and that people had to tighten their belts.

At this time Martin O'Donoghue was sketching together a Draft called 'The Economic Emergency', which was a paper that included a programme for job creation, tax cuts etc. The day after the Election was called Fianna Fáil launched the final printed document, called 'The Manifesto', which caught the Government by surprise, appealed to the people who were tired of belt tightening and dominated the whole campaign from then on. O'Donoghue had also worked out a strategy to defeat the Tullymander being of the opinion that mathematically, a swing of 2.2% would attain victory. A lot of credit must also be given to Seamus Brennan who behind the scenes in those opposition years was restructuring the party, started a youth movement and introduced new, young blood as candidates. An exhausting tour of the country by Lynch himself, which involved many sorties into convents and religious institutions helped the 'Honest Jack' image, together with a simple slogan – 'Let's back Jack', and 'The Real Taoiseach', put the icing on the cake and brought Fianna Fail back to power with a majority of twenty seats, their biggest majority ever. O'Donoghue himself became a last-minute candidate, accompanying David Andrews on the Dun Laoghaire ticket, and was duly elected.

Now back in power, Jack continued the inner circle of advisors and began to run the country in a sort of presidential style. Though Colley was made Minister for Finance, some of his powers were taken over by Martin O'Donoghue as Minister in the newly created Department of Economic Planning and Development. Haughey, surprisingly, was given the Social Welfare portfolio, along with the Health portfolio, two high-budget and influential Departments and a good balance with Colley's now diluted Department of Finance. O'Donoghue took no time at all to establish himself as a force within the Cabinet. Early in his Ministry, he obtained a number of concessions passed at Cabinet level that gave him very wide powers, especially for dealing with Trades Unions – a liberty he was able to use when negotiating with the Unions and one they admitted was welcome. It gave him great power over his civil servants and even enabled him to renegotiate policy already settled by Cabinet. This free hand however, got him at loggerheads with other Ministers, especially Charlie Haughey when he attempted to raise the health eligibility ceiling. Haughey had worked very hard and had got a good deal with the doctors and O'Donoghue was now interfering in Haughey's Department, which angered Haughey no end. O'Donoghue got his way. Then, under the Programme for National Understanding. He introduced the idea of a National Employment Agency, which was in essence cutting across the I.D.A. in Des O'Malley's new Ministry of Industry and Commerce. Fianna Fáil had rubbished a similar idea by the Coalition. While O'Malley was on a trade mission to China, O'Donoghue again got his way. He then came up against Colley in Finance when he tried to bring in reform in the Civil Service. He delayed this part of his brief until 1979 but came up against strong opposition. As stated already, Jack Lynch was operating within a very tight circle of, worst of all, the Cabinet sub-committee on the economy which handled all the important issues in economic policy. This committee was made up of Lynch, O'Donoghue, Colley, O'Malley, Gibbons and Fitzgerald, but it had an even smaller inner circle that became known as the 'gang of four', of Lynch, O'Donoghue, Colley and O'Malley. This cosy cartel of an administration seemed to work fairly well in 1978, which was a remarkable year by any standards, probably the best record any Government had in the history of the State. 20,000 jobs were created, the economy grew by 7% and inflation was halved to 13%.

The fact that a number of economic decisions were now being taken by the 'gang of four', or at most the sub-committee on the economy and only requiring rubber-stamping by the full Cabinet angered the rest of the Cabinet, especially Haughey. The lack of information coming back to the Cabinet became very apparent in the negotiation for the country's entry into the EMS (European Monetary System). The negotiations were carried out at various stages by the Departments of Foreign Affairs, Finance and Economic Planning and Development. With Britain's objection to the scheme at the Brussels summit in December 1978, Ireland's negotiation became somewhat confused. This happened especially in regard to the compensation package that Ireland were to receive, in which there was confusion as to whether it was £45 million for five years, or per year for five years. This also led to the media getting it wrong and O'Donoghue had to go on radio to contradict the newspapers, and in doing so appeared to contradict Lynch's version of the story. In the end O'Donoghue played no small part in sorting out the problem and ensuring Ireland's entry and compensation package. By the end of 1978 things seemed to be running smoothly for the Government, apart form an apparent Balance of Payments problem and possible spiraling inflation from the National Understanding agreement worked out with the social partners in May of that year. 40,000 jobs achieved since they came into power, albeit mostly in the public sector, seemed a good omen for the coming year. However, this was not to be so, especially for Jack Lynch.

In his February Budget of 1979, Minister for Finance, George Colley, in order to bring the farming community into the tax net, attempted to impose a 2% levy on all agricultural produce. This was out of the blue, even to the backbench T.D.s and one of them, Tom Meany from Mid-Cork tabled a motion against the levy. At the parliamentary meeting, though there was a lot of criticism of the tax, it was finally accepted with modifications, which included exemption for milk produce under 5,000 gallons (Tom McEllistrim, N. Kerry), beet produce exempted, (Mark Killilea, Galway E.) and others who wanted pigs, sheep and cattle slaughtered under the Disease Eradication Scheme exempt. On the eve of the Ard Fheis, Colley succumbed to the above modifications with changes whereby milk would be exempt up to 5,000 gallons and only beet produced west of the Shannon would be omitted. Though there were still reservations in the farming community and the issue seemed to be put to rest, Colley surprised everybody at a meeting with the farming organisations, where he was accompanied by the Taoiseach, Jack Lynch and Agricultural Minister Gibbons in the following week, when he dropped the levy completely until a fair system of taxation was worked out with the farmers. O'Donoghue absented himself from this meeting as he was against the measure in the first place. The backbenchers were caught flatfooted again as they had spent the weekend in their constituencies selling the idea of the new levy. But this was not to be the only problem. The PAYE sector of the community, who had for some time been complaining of their share of tax they were contributing to the Government's kitty, now seeing the Government giving in once more to the farmers decided to take to the streets in numbers approaching a million. With the attempted levy of 2%, the Government, one could say, had upset the whole population.

The next nail in Lynch's coffin was the postal strike, which lasted five months and Minister for Post & Telegraphs, Padraig Faulkner's rigid stand on the pay issue added to the already aggrieved public. His excuse that he was restricted in addressing pay claims in the postal service by the Coalition's embargo on special increases in public servants' pay in 1975 did not wear with the public, as was realised in the poor results obtained by Fianna Fáil in the June Local and European Elections. I, the author, can vouch for this personally as I was a Fianna Fáil candidate in the local election in Wicklow.

Another factor to add to the backbenchers' grievances was how

Jack Lynch handled Jim Gibbons' ignoring the three-line whip on the second reading of Charlie Haughey's Family Planning Bill. His excuse that his views on contraception were well known did not solve the problem at the next parliamentary meeting and Jack Lynch said he would handle it personally. Two meetings of the Taoiseach and Gibbons came to nothing, and backbenchers who were expecting a sacking for Gibbons as Minister, or withdrawal of the whip, were totally surprised, and again there was further proof that Lynch did not have full control of his Cabinet. As Gibbons had defied Lynch on a number of occasions since the Arms Trial and in view of the latest revelations that we now know, was there some reason why Lynch was unable to discipline Gibbons? Whatever the reason, the backbenchers were getting uneasy as it had dropped its share of the vote in the European elections from 50.6% in 1977 to 34.6%, the lowest recorded vote they had ever got. Obviously a swing of this nature would unseat a lot of Deputies and more than likely put the Coalitions back in power in a General Election. Nothing focuses a T.D. like the possibility of losing his seat in the next election.

The main grievances as experienced by the candidates on the doorsteps during the elections were the farm levy fiasco, the PAYE question, the ongoing Post Office strike, rising inflation and oil prices. When these problems were brought up at a parliamentary meeting by worried backbenchers, their concerns were brushed aside as a mid-term blip. The lack of communication between the inner sanctum of the 'gang of four' and the backbenchers one could say, was responsible for the creation of the 'Gang of Five', as the leaders of the anti-Lynch campaign came to be known. The movement started in Jury's Coffee Dock when Tom McEllistrim (N. Kerry) and Jackie Fahey (Waterford), roped in Albert Reynolds (Longford/Westmeath) and Sean Doherty (Roscommon/Leitrim) in late night discussions into taking action to solve the problem. Feelers went out to others that had good reason were of the same mind. The circle widened, taking in Ray McSharry (Sligo/Leitrim), Mark Killilea (Galway East), Padraig Flynn (Mayo West), Charlie McCreevy (Kildare) and Senators Bernard McGlinchey and Flor Crowley. Later still Paddy Power, Síle De Valera, Bill Loughnane and Seán Calleary widened the group further.

Ray McSharry. Minister for Agriculture, Minister for Finance and EEC Commissioner.

On the evening of the parliamentary party that ignored the grievances of the backbenchers, five of the above met in the coffee Dock in Jury's and retired to Tom McEllistrim's room to discuss the dilemma. The five were: Tom McEllistrim, Jackie Fahey, Sean Doherty, Albert Reynolds and Mark Killelea, and these five became know as the 'Gang of Five'.

During the time that all these things were happening Charlie Haughey was carving out a reputation for himself as an excellent Minister for Health and Social Welfare. As Shadow Minister for Health in opposition he had been more than able to take on a lacklustre Minister for Health, Brendan Corish. Now with the reins in his hands he showed that his criticisms of Corish when in opposition were no empty challenges. He initiated schemes to help the elderly which included free bottled gas and free telephone rental. He increase the Social Welfare budget by £55 million and the Health budget by £45 million and created 2,400 jobs in the process. His promotion of health, through the Health Education bureau informing the public by an excellent media campaign to improve their heath and fitness by jogging, running, dancing, playing games, giving up smoking, cutting down on alcohol and walking instead of driving. To show the way he gave up cigarettes and alcohol himself. He introduced legislation to give him power over the methods that companies had for advertising cigarettes and banned sponsorship from cigarettes in certain areas. He provided the finance for the building of the new Beaumont hospital, the new Cork Regional hospital and development and extensions to hospitals in Mullingar and Sligo, as well as initiating the building of a new general hospital in Tralee. He introduced a free hospitalisation scheme for all people earning less than £5,500 per annum, which was not included in the Manifesto. He approved measures to improve the pay, conditions and status of nurses. He also introduced the Family Planning Bill. This was all coming to the notice of the public and in an opinion poll asking preferences for Taoiseach at the time of the passing of the Bill through the Dáil, Haughey, with 75%, came top of the list, even above Lynch, with Colley and Faulkner at the bottom. Dissolution with Lynch's leadership became more widespread and sabres began to rattle within the party.

On August 27th, Lord Mountbatten was murdered while boating at Mullochmore, Co. Sligo, and this, together with the mass murder of eighteen British soldiers at Warrenpoint, brought Anglo-Irish relations to a low ebb. While attending the funeral of Mountbatten in London, Lynch had a summit meeting with British Prime Minister, Margaret Thatcher, where they agreed security arrangements which were to have repercussions for Lynch within the party a short time later. During the visit of Pope John Paul II in early September, rumours circulated that the President, Paddy Hillary, was going to resign due to an alleged scandal that he was having an affair. He subsequently called a Press Conference denying the charge. Rumour had it later still that the original rumour had been spread by people who believed Hillary was stepping down as President so that he could become leader of Fianna Fáil and by some political or constitutional wizardry become Taoiseach. However, Síle De Valera is reputed to have started the ball rolling with a speech in Fermoy on September 9th in which she criticised Lynch's Northern policy. Lynch had earlier seen the speech and had advised her that parts of it were not appropriate at that time. She, however, gave the unedited speech and defended it at a subsequent Parliamentary meeting, receiving a good backing from many at the meeting. This was followed a month later by Tom McEllistrim when he criticised a Government decision to allow British military aircraft to over fly the border in an agreed corridor to follow subversives and put down a motion for the parliamentary party meeting. It was believed that Lynch had gone too soft with Thatcher due to the death of Mountbatten. McEllistrim agreed to withdraw the motion on assurances from Lynch that the air corridor would not infringe on Irish Sovereignty. However, Jack Lynch, in an interview with the *Washington Post* in the USA admitted that the security deal would have no changes with regard to air control regulations on overflights. With that, Dr. Bill Loughnane called the Taoiseach a liar and George Colley, acting-Taoiseach while Lynch was away, called a Parliamentary meeting with a motion to remove the whip from Loughnane. After a day-long meeting Colley failed to oust Loughnane.

The loss of two Bye-elections in Cork, Jack Lynch's own back garden, were the final nails in Lynch's coffin. If the backbenchers were worried about losing their seats in the next election before, this copper fastened their fears. A petition was organised to ascertain the Deputies who were in favour of getting rid of Lynch. Vincent Brown, in an article *The making of a Taoiseach*, in January 1980, lists from information he had got the list of twenty as being:- Liam Aylward, Lorcan Allen, Johnny Callanan. Sean Calleary, Ger Connelly, Brendan Crinnion, Brendan Daly, Síle De Valera, Sean Dogherty, Jackie Fahey, Padraig Flynn, Joe Fox, Sean Keegan, Mark Killilea, Eileen Lemass, Bill Loughnane, Charlie McGreevy, Tom McEllistrim, Ray McSharry, Chub O'Connor and Paddy Power.

When Jack Lynch returned from the USA he brought up the subject of a caucus meeting he had heard of and enquired who was there. Only Padraig Flynn admitted his involvement. With this wall of silence Lynch knew the writing was on the wall and though he had already decided to go in January of 1980, with assurances from Colley and O'Donoghue that if a snap election was called it would take Haughey supporters by surprise and give Colley a better chance of wining. Lynch announced his resignation on December 5th and called an election for two days later. It goes to show how little Colley's main canvassers – Molloy, O'Donoghue, Willie Kennelly, Joe Farrell and Des O'Malley – knew the situation on the ground or what was happening around them. Haughey's main canvassers, McEllistrim and Killilea, had tied up the backbenchers and with Michael O'Kennedy and, it is believed, Brian Lenihan the only Ministers voting for Haughey, he defeated Colley by 44 votes to 38 and became leader of Fianna Fáil and Taoiseach. Colley's naivety led him to believe that with the majority of the Cabinet behind him he was home and dry. People like O'Malley and Molloy, as Ministers had cut themselves off from their fellow Deputies and O'Donoghue, a newcomer and Minister form day one were not in touch with what was happening due to the Presidential type of leadership that Lynch had adopted. The victory was a brilliant stroke for the backbenchers and democracy in general and it is believed that the main benefactor, Charles J. Haughey, had very little involvement in the coup – up to a very close to the end at least.

The author, Donal O'Shea pictured with Noel Dempsey, Minister for Marine and Natural Resources and Séamus Brennan, Minister for Social and Family Affairs.

Charles J. Haughey – The Early Years

Charles J. Haughey was born in Castlebar on 16th September 1925. both his parents came from Swatteragh, Co. Derry. His father, Johnny, was active in the War of Independence and though a staunch republican, after the Treaty he joined the Free State army and is reputed to have taken guns over the border for Michael Collins. He obviously believed in Collins' idea of the Treaty being a stepping-stone to a United Ireland. He was to learn however, that after Collins' death that the survivors had little interest in the North, and in 1928 he retired from the army and bought a small farm in Dunshaughlin, Co. Meath. He was, however, struck down with multiple sclerosis and he had to give up the farm and move to Dublin, where he took up residence at Belton Park Road. Due to his illness he was unable to work and his wife had to bring up seven children on an army pension and a small IRA pension. Charlie went to school in Marino, where he progressed very well and obtained a Dublin Corporation Scholarship. From there he advanced to St. Joseph's CBS in Fairview where he excelled academically and sportswise, achieving a Dublin County Council Scholarship to University College Dublin and was selected for the Leinster Colleges in both hurling and football. He was later to win a Dublin County Championship medal in football with Parnells. His classmates at St. Joseph's included Harry Boland and George Colley. In U.C.D. he took a B. Comm. Degree in 1946 and went on to qualify as an accountant. He was also called to the Bar, a profession he never practised. While at U.C.D. He was Auditor of the Commerce Society. It was at U.C.D. Also that he showed his first signs of his republican spirit. He and a number of other students burnt the Union Jack in front of Trinity College in retaliation for Trinity students burning the Tri-Colour because passers-by had complained that the Tri-Colour was flying below the flags of the other Allies in Trinity's celebrations of the defeat of Germany in the Second World War. The whole incident disintegrated into a messy situation and received widespread publicity. Having obtained his accountancy qualifications he joined Harry Boland and together they set up the Haughey & Boland firm of Accountants. While at U.C.D. his contemporary students included Garret Fitzgerald, Joan O'Farrell, who Fitzgerald later married, and Maureen Lemass, daughter of the later Taoiseach. In 1951 he married Maureen Lemass and between 1955 and 1961 they had four children – Eimear, Conor, Ciarán and Seán. Around the time of their marriage they moved into a house in Raheny. In 1957, they moved to an old Victorian mansion on forty-five acres of land in Grangemore. They sold this to Mat Gallagher in 1959 and bought the Kinsealy mansion, a home of former Lord Lieutenants, where they lived ever since. His first taste of public life was when he was co-opted onto Dublin Corporation having failed as a Dáil candidate in the General Election in 1951. Having again failed to make the Dáil in the General Election of 1954 and a Bye-election in 1956, he was eventually elected to Dáil Éireann in the General Election of 1957.

He made an immediate impact in a Dáil Éireann, the majority of whose Cabinet had been around for a long time and were getting quite old. In his early speeches he showed great talent and foresight in advocating Advance Factories, which could be leased out to prospective entrepreneurs, an idea that was later introduced by the I.D.A. He proposed that companies needed more profits as a motivation to expand and thus create more employment and that more State involvement and investment was required. He suggested that more research was needed in agriculture to enable farming to become more profitable and that Bord Iascaigh Mhara needed to introduce long-term downstream industries like boat building, pier construction and fish processing. He did, even at this time, cross swords in Dáil debates with such experienced orators as James Dillon and Oliver O'Flanagan. On one occasion in a discussion on costs, the young accountant/Deputy told Dillon that he was a better orator than a mathematician and in another debate he retorted to Dillon's reference to his long years of experience in the Dáil as that the Deputy had "gone a little senile". There was no doubt but that this young man was going to go places and so it was only a matter of time, when it was decided that the ageing Minister for Justice, Oscar Traynor, now 75, needed a Parliamentary Secretary, that the young Haughey was the man. Though suggested by Traynor, in Haughey's own constituency, Lemass was not totally in favour of it and advised Haughey that as Taoiseach he was offering him the job and as his father-in-law he was advising him to refuse it. Haughey, however, accepted the position and took over that part of Traynor's duties which guided Bills through their various stages in the Dáil. His first task in this area was to take five Bills that had already gone through their first stage through to enactment. These were: The Charities Bill, 1957; The Solicitor' (Amendment) Bill, 1960; The Rent Restriction's Bill, 1960; The Civil Liability Bill, 1960 and the Defamation Bill, 1961. His dexterity in piloting Bills through the Dáil gained the ultimate compliment from the leader of the opposition, James Dillon, when he stated ". . . I compliment him on the skill with which he has recourse to his brief. He has read out to the house learned discourses on various aspects of this legislation which, I have no doubt, will be quoted from the Official Reports hereafter as evidence of his exceptional and outstanding ability". John Healy, in an article in *In Dublin* in 1986 stated that ". . . anybody reading the now fading back copies of the Dáil debates will see, almost from his first day in Parliament, the evidence of a quick sharp mind, constructive and positive in approaching constituency problems".

1961 saw a General Election and the retirement of Oscar Traynor. Charlie Haughey headed the poll with 8,566 votes in an election that saw Fianna Fail take three out of five seats in Haughey's constituency; George Colley and Eugene Timmons being the other two.

Donal O'Shea and Charles Haughey 1987.

Haughey – His first Ministry is Justice

When the votes were counted after the 1961 General Election, Fianna Fáil were short five seats for an overall majority, but with two Independents voting with the outgoing Taoiseach, and one Independent abstaining, Lemass was again installed as Taoiseach, and Fianna Fáil returned with a Minority Government. Lemass, in his appointments to the Cabinet, went more or less with the same personnel with the exception of Oscar Traynor, who had retired. Charlie Haughey's appointment as Minister for Justice was one of the few appointments that was not criticised by the opposition in what they described as a rather dull lot. In fact, Fine Gael Deputy, Michael J. O'Higgins congratulated Lemass on Haughey's appointment, stating that, "I have no doubt it will improve the team which the Taoiseach has suggested to the House.

Haughey lost no time in bringing in reforms in legislation, especially social reform legislation. In his first day in the Ministry, he introduced two pieces of legislation, The Coroner's Bill and the Garda Siochana Bill. At this time the Gardaí were becoming restless due to low pay, poor prospects of promotion and lack of leadership. When a pay demand from the Garda Representative body was turned down, disillusioned members held meeting in barracks in Dublin, but they were banned from using the premises by the Commissioner. They then decided to have a rally at the Macushla Ballroom and Haughey directed that they were not to go ahead with it. This direction was defied and they came up with a go-slow campaign. Haughey responded by dismissing eleven of the ringleaders. At the same time, he did however agree to look into the grievances if the Commissioner could guarantee that "discipline had been restored." A secret meeting of Haughey and the Catholic Archbishop of Dublin, John Charles McQuaid, then one of the most powerful influences in the country, was followed by a statement by the Archbishop that discipline would be restored if the grievances were investigated by the Department of Justice. This in turn was followed by a statement by Haughey that the investigation would be carried out. He also restored the eleven Gardai that had been dismissed and all other proceedings were dropped. It was the first time that the loyalty of the force could no longer be taken for granted.

Very early in his Ministry he drew up a plan for his term of his Ministry. He was the first to recognise that the IRA's campaign in the North had failed and that the IRA were demoralised. In November he reactivated the Special Criminal Courts, dormant since World War II, and started handing out stiff sentences to any member of the IRA who were prosecuted for any offence. At the same time he offered an amnesty to those that would hand over their weapons – long before the decommissioning requirements of the Good Friday agreement of more recent times, and when the IRA publicly called off their campaign he responded positively by disbanding the Special Criminal Courts and releasing prisoners held under that law.

Prior to Haughey's term as Minister, it was the custom to fix cases where politicians or their friends were caught for drunken driving. Haughey refused to go along with this and organised a system whereby the culprit would not get any publicity. Friendly Judges would arise, leave the court and go to their rooms as if the session was ended for the day and when the reporters went home, the judge would return, the defendants would plead guilty and take their punishment, but the result would never reach the newspapers as the reporters had to be present in court in order to report it. John Healy was quite annoyed at this, so when Donagh O'Malley was pulled for drunken driving, Healy reported it as headline news in the final edition of the then *Daily Mail*. That ended the secret courts. Attempts to transfer the Garda who brought O'Malley to court was raised in the Dáil by Fine Gael, but was thwarted when Haughey promised to expose Fine Gael with the threat that, "There are some quare files in my Department too" – a technique John O'Donoghue was to use as Minister for Justice in 2,000 when his driver was pulled up for driving the State car well over the speed limit. During his period in Justice he focussed mainly on replacing antiquated laws with law that, ". . . as far as possible . . . be contained in modern statutes passed by the Oireachtas", and that this in time would apply "to all our statute law". With that in mind he continued introducing new Bills, amending some and re-enacting others. Some of the most interesting Bills were the Criminal Justice Bill and The Succession Bill, while some of the more difficult were: The Courts (Supplementary Provisions Amendment) Bill, and the Intoxicating Liquor Bill. The main features of the Criminal Justice Bill of 1963 were the abolition of Capital Punishment, except in the case of the murder of a Garda, the assassination of an ambassador or treason, exceptions that were finally removed from the statute book by a referendum on the Treaty of Nice in 2001. Up to the Succession Bill, a man could cut his wife and family out of his will and leave his possessions to anyone or any cause he wished. The Act compelled him to leave one third of his wealth to his wife, one third to his children and he was free to do what he liked with the final third.

Haughey came up against the opposition in the case of the Intoxicating Liquor Bill of 1962, even though it considered only minor adjustments to the licensing hours, while provisions to increase substantially the salaries of members of the judiciary in the Courts (Supplemental Provisions Amendment) Act also brought an outcry from the opposition. With the latter, Haughey maintained that the increase was necessary to attract the best people and put the objection from the opposition down to begrudgery. He showed great compassion for prisoners and though he maintained that prisons should be places of punishment, they should be "places of rehabilitation" as well. The Firearms Bill, The Guardianship of Infants Bill and the Adoption Bill showed his concern for children; the first regulating the use of airguns, the second increased the age from seven to nine for a child to be adopted and extended the right of adoption to non-Irish parents, while the latter Bills stipulated that the child is to be the first consideration. With juvenile crime reaching its highest levels in the early sixties, Haughey introduced the Special Garda Crime Unit and a Juvenile liaison scheme whereby, under Garda supervision and with the co-operation of parents, teachers, youth leaders or other guardians, an offending youth could avoid being put in a penal institute. In addition at that time, Archbishop McQuaid provided, free of charge, an after-care institution for young people. Institutions like these however have in recent years been exposed as places where children were subjected to terrible abuse, including sexual abuse.

The Criminal Justice (Legal Aid) Bill provided free legal aid to people who the court decided was "essential, in the interest of justice". Other Bills he piloted through the Oireachtas during his term were the Short Titles Bill, the Official Streets Bill, Statute Law Revision (Pre-Union Irish Statutes) Bill, Hotel Proprietors Bill, Registration of Titles Bill, Funds of Suitors Bill, Courts (1963) Bill, Pawnbrokers Bill, Extradition Bill, and the Civil Liberties (Amendment) Bill. Though completely immersed in his own Department, he did find time to contribute his compassionate nature when he strongly defended the introduction of a $2\frac{1}{2}\%$ Turnover sales tax in the Budget of 1963 when he stated that it would provide finance for an increase in Welfare Payments and Children's Allowances as there was no other source of monies available to do so. During his term in Justice he got excellent help from Roger Hayes, who was also interested in law reform. However, a number of problems arose between Haughey and Peter Berry, Secretary of the Department, particularly in the area of selection of personnel. Berry was very set in his ways as he had been in the Department for a number of years and this at times clashed with Haughey's willingness to get things done quickly. Towards the end of 1964 Paddy Smith, Minister for Agriculture, resigned from office as he did not agree with Lemass's economic policies, feeling that he was giving too much attention to urban and industrial areas and not enough to rural and agriculture. To avoid a crisis that might topple a Minority Government, Lemass speedily appointed a replacement from within the Cabinet, making Charlie Haughey the new Minister for Agriculture and taking over Justice himself. This was a surprise choice as Haughey, being a city man, people believed that he would not have the relevant knowledge and experience to operate the Agriculture Portfolio. Haughey, however, dismissed this in the Dáil by stating that he owned a profitable chicken farm in Co. Meath. If that was not enough, a trip to the west of Ireland with senior officials from his Department, Brian Lenihan and journalist, John Healy, where he visited farms throughout Roscommon and Mayo, were an added baptism for Haughey in the needs of farmers throughout the country.

The author, Donal O'Shea pictured with Séamus Brennan, Minister for Social and Family Affairs, Cllr. Frank Chambers and his wife Phil.

Haughey in Agriculture

Though the *modus operandi* and application of the Agriculture was much different to that in Justice, Haughey went straight down to business. He pushed the promotion of the Heifer/Calf Scheme that had been introduced by Paddy Smith, and introduced Farrow/Sow and Hogget/Ewe Schemes to increase the stocks of cattle, pigs and sheep in the country. He imported Friesian and Charolais cattle, Texel sheep from The Netherlands and pigs from Scandinavia to improve the national breeds.

He continued strenuously the scheme for the eradication of Bovine T.B., introduced a new scheme for the eradication of brucellosis and planned new veterinary laboratories for Athlone, Cork, Limerick and Sligo to complement the existing one in Meath. He advocated more training and further education which he believed would produce more successful farmers and he introduced more research programmes to expand farming into other areas like horse breeding and glasshouse farming and he set up a committee to improve the woollen industry.

By the end of the second year of his Ministry he was able to boast an increase in the national herd to 1.5 million, increases in pigs going to slaughter, poultry of 15% each and that the Bovine T.B. Eradication testing was completed. The only blip was a drop in tillage, due to bad weather. The rise in farm income by 5% in 1965 however, hid the fact that 45,000 had left farming between 1964 and 1966. Ominous signs were beginning to creep into the farming economy in that though the national herds were increasing, protectionist policies being pursued by the EEC and EFTA (European Free Trade Association) were reducing the market and causing surpluses in Ireland, with consequential effects on prices. Haughey felt that the situation would be remedied by the Anglo-Irish Free Trade Agreement, which Lemass, Lynch and himself had negotiated, and was due to come into effect in June. The terms of this agreement as far as agriculture was concerned was a doubling of our butter quota to the UK, free access for our store cattle to that market and an extension to the British agricultural support price system to our finished products, 25,000 tons of carcass beef and 5,500 tons of carcass lamb. All in all, the whole agreement would be worth about £10 million per annum.

During this time the N.F.A. and the I.C.M.S.A. were beginning to show their strength. They were both competing for dairy farmers that were unattached to any organisation and they used various promotional tactics in continuously trying to outdo each other. In the Spring they sought from the Government a price increase structure that was two-tiered; all farmers would get an increase of 4d per gallon for the first 7,000 gallons per annum and an extra 2d for any produced above that quota. Haughey refused to meet this request, stating that though he would like to help the farmers, the cost of £6 million could not be afforded by the Government. This resulted in the I.C.M.S.A. leader, John Feely, placing an illegal picket outside Leinster House on 27th April 1966. The Government's reaction was to have 186 I.C.M.S.A. members arrested over the next three days under the Offences Against the State Act. Eventually Haughey agreed to meet them to discuss "other ways in which the incomes of farmers can be increased". Their demands were still the same and Haughey was wary that by giving in, he would be further making the farmers more dependent on the State and not as his intention was for them to "achieve self-reliant, independent and progressive agriculture, fully backed by, but not utterly dependent by the State".

However, give in he did, by offering them an immediate price increase of 2d, with a further increase for quality milk after April 1st, 1967. As they already got 1d increase only recently, this meant that if the quality was right, they had in fact got the 4d increase they were looking for. This, however, might have something to do with the fact that Haughey was Director of Elections for the forthcoming Presidential Election and it would not be a good idea to have the rural community up in arms against Fianna Fáil. As it turned out, it was the right decision politically wise, as De Valera only narrowly defeated Fine Gael's Tom O'Higgins, the election being clinched in the rural areas after a tough fight in Dublin.

In the summer, the price of cattle collapsed, mostly due to external factors, and as 80% of our market was in exports, there was very little the Department could do. The main factors involved were a prohibitive tariff introduced by the EEC on non-members, a sea strike in the UK, a glut on the market after the sea strike and a credit squeeze in the UK, which prevented British farmers keeping Irish cattle for the two months necessary to claim a subsidy from their Government. The ongoing battle for supremacy between the I.C.M.S.A., the N.F.A. and the Irish Beet grower's Association, the fact that Haughey had given in to the I.C.M.S.A. on the milk price issue in the run up to the Presidential Election; and that Lemass had given his intention to step down as Taoiseach caused Ricard Deasy, head of the N.F.A. to start rattling cages. Deasy led a large band of farmers in a famous march from the West of Ireland to Merrion Street, the back entrance to the Dáil. Many groups joined the march from many parts of the country, so that by the time it reached Dublin it was quite a formidable mob. Merrion Street was all railed off with a large contingent of Gardai manning the barricades. Lemass backed Haughey in not meeting with them, as in so doing it would be giving in to their bullying tactics and opening the way for other non-democratic groups eroding the powers of a duly elected Government, leading to anarchy. Deasy, now in an embarrassing position, took a small delegation of eight through the barricades to meet the Minister. He was denied an interview and so they squatted on the steps of Agriculture House, stating they would not leave until they had a meeting with the Minister. This went on for weeks. In the meantime, Haughey headed for Europe, trawling the various countries looking for markets for cattle. The only luck he had was an order for 2,000 head from Germany, which he prematurely announced in the Dáil before his German colleagues had discussed with their fellow European partners in the EEC. During this period Haughey was subject to a number of attacks on his car; once in Athlone and twice at the Intercontinental Hotel in Dublin.

In October 1966, Lemass suddenly decided to step down as Taoiseach, which led to the famous succession stakes. This took the wind out of the farmers' rally and focus now turned on who would be the next leader of Fianna Fáil and Taoiseach. Lemass and Haughey met the farmers and promised them that their issues would be taken up by the new administration and the protest was called off. As we learned in the Jack Lynch part of our history, after an initial flurry by Colley, Haughey and Blaney for the leadership, Lemass, in the interest of party unity asked Jack Lynch to go forward. When Lynch reluctantly did, Haughey and Blaney pulled out of the race and Jack Lynch defeated George Colley by fifty-two votes to nineteen. Haughey was elevated to Minister for Finance in the new Government.

Haughey is now Number Two

Charlie Haughey had now attained the number two Ministry at a time when the country was doing very well economically and Ministers, especially like the 'Three Musketeers' of Haughey, Donagh O'Malley and Brian Lenihan, plus Blaney and Boland, being given plenty of scope for individualism by Lynch. This particularly suited Haughey and Blaney who had strong ambitions for the Number One job, believing that Lynch was only an interim Taoiseach. Haughey presented an excellent first budget on March 31st, with a surplus of £800,000 against Minister of Finance Lynch's budget of the previous year, with a deficit of £8 million. He was also able to reverse Lynch's Deflationary Measures of 1966. He sought no tax for Capital items, preferring instead to finance same by borrowing at home and abroad. He increased Government spending on Local Authority Housing by £12.5 million, including £3 million for the 'Seven Towers' high-rise housing estate in Ballymun. He blamed the rise in unemployment on a falling emigration due to bad economic conditions in the UK. The usual increases on the 'old reliables' of drink, cigarettes and petrol were psychologically matched by concessions for the elderly in the form of free ESB, telephone and travel for old-age pensioners. He never forgot the hardship his mother suffered in rearing seven of them with meagre monies, when her husband became ill and later died. He got rid of rates on poor agricultural land and introduced unemployment assistance or the 'farmer's dole' to any farmer whose valuation was under £5, which was 10,000 smallholders. Politically, this helped to improve his relationship with the farming community that was damaged during his tenure as Minister for Agriculture.

Haughey had a great interest in the American political campaign style of electioneering. He encouraged Des McGreevey to set up a 'ways and means' fund-raising body. This was to become known as TACA, which was a system whereby businessmen would contribute £100 per head each year to the election fund and the money would be banked in a deposit account until election time and the interest made on it in the meantime would be spent on special dinners where the contributors would get a chance to meet and discuss their various concerns with the Ministers in an informal way. It would bring about a levelling of contributors across the many contributors to the party, some of which would have been much greater than £100. At the first dinner organised by Blaney, the whole Cabinet were present, each one at a different table. The opposition accused the Government of possibilities of corruption as a large number of the contributors were big builders and land developers and felt that deals were being done by the Government in renting premises being developed and built by these people. They failed to realise that most builders favoured Fianna Fáil in Government as it was always a good Government for initiating policies that encouraged the building of houses, offices and factories as well as road development. Matt Gallagher, the builder, always maintained that Fianna Fáil was good for builders and builders were good for Fianna Fáil. At around this time George Colley made his famous statement about 'low standards in high places', which most people felt was aimed at Haughey, but which Colley later said was referring to the opposition.

In May 1967 Ireland applied for membership of the EEC and a delegation was set up to meet the existing six members. It was made up of Lynch, Haughey and two Department Secretaries, T. K . Whittiger, (Finance) and Hugh McCann (Foreign Affairs). The key advantages of going into the EEC at the time were explained by Haughey as it would get rid of the enormous expense to the Exchequer of subsidizing the export of surplus agricultural goods as well as helping us to be more secure within the larger union. It was always agreed however that due to our large dependence on the UK for our trade, we could not go in if Britain stayed out. This dependence was well demonstrated by our having to devalue our currency by 14.3%, similar to the UK, when Britain devalued in November of 1967. In Haughey's Budget of April 1968 he reported that the cost of living had gone up by 2%. He introduced Pensions for the widows of T.D.s and Senators and he increased Deputies salaries form £1,500 to £2,500 and Ministerial salaries by the same ratio. 1969 was election year and preparations for this started in 1968 when Kevin Boland got the job of the revision of constituencies and in his endeavours to attain an overall majority for Fianna Fail he introduced a Referendum to abolish Proportional Representation and replace it with the single seat system. However, like in 1959 it was again defeated. This setback was, however, balanced by Haughey's Budget in 1969 which increased Children's Allowances, subsided petrol for disabled drivers, gave income tax exemptions for artists and writers, as well as £100 and £150 respectively to parents of triplets and quadruplets. Haughey was appointed National Director of Elections. He produced an excellent American-style campaign, with Lynch doing a whistle-stop tour of the country. Though Labour had some very high profile candidates in Conor Cruise O'Brien, Justin Keating, Dr. Noel Brown and David Thornley promoting, 'The seventies will be socialist', a counterpromotion of 'Reds under the bed', plus an exploitation of the differences between Labour and Fine Gael and a demonstration of the failure of previous Coalitions ensured that Fianna Fail were returned to power with their first overall majority since 1957. the events that took place following the 1969 election victory – the outbreak of the troubles in the North, the Arms Trial, the sacking of Charley Haughey and Neil Blaney, plus Haughey's ten-year strategy that brought him to the position of Taoiseach have been covered in the Lynch years.

Haughey's First Term as Taoiseach

Haughey's first task as Taoiseach was to make amends and try to unite the party. He did this by reappointing most of the Ministers of the previous Government, all of which, with the exception of Lenihan, had voted against him in the leadership contest. At his first press conference after his election he stated that the party had pledged their loyalty to him. George Colley, who he had appointed as Tánaiste, told the Parliamentary Party that he did not pledge this loyalty, and this action, plus Colley's conspiring against the Government, prompted Bruce Arnold, no friend of Haughey's, to state that this was unconstitutional and intolerable. He did drop Martin O'Donoghue and scrapped his Department of Economic Planning, a function he then took under his own wing in the Department of the Taoiseach. The dropping of O'Donoghue was no surprise as Haughey never though much of the Manifesto of 1977 which was O'Donoghue's baby. The peculiar thing about O'Donoghue and Desmond O'Malley, who were all proponents of financial rectitude in the early '80s, as the 'Gang of Four' in Lynch's Cabinet, were the main driving force for the Manifesto, which was one of the main causes of the financial problems in the first place. Albert Reynolds was the only member of the 'Gang of Five' who took the initiative to replace Lynch with Haughey to be rewarded with a senior Cabinet post in Post & Telegraphs. In order to exert more control over all departments, Haughey proceeded to expand two-fold and later, threefold, the office of Taoiseach. On the Economic front, Haughey gave his famous television talk to the nation on 10th January, 1980, in which he stated that, "As a community we have been living at a rate which is simply not justified by the amount of goods and services we are producing. To make up the difference we have been borrowing enormous amounts of money, ... at a rate that cannot continue". This philosophy differed, however, with his own personal financial affairs.

Between late 1971 and the time he became Taoiseach, he had increased his own borrowings from £244,000 to £1.1 million by late 1979; this in view of the fact that it bore no resemblance to what would appear to be his ability to pay back, as a politician's salary would not justify that amount of borrowings.

John Healy did try, in an article in *In Dublin* in October 1986, to explain how Haughey would have acquired the wherewithal to be able to do this. "Haughey", he stated, "was to see what poor rewards there were for a life in politics, but long before that he had, himself, determined as a young articled accountancy man he would make £100,000 before he was thirty. It was like a twenty-year-old promising to make a million by the turn of the century". As it was perceived that Haughey was to be the saviour of the economy, various businessmen decided to come to his aid as it was felt that they should help him get his finances in order. Matt Gallagher had always said that Fianna Fáil was good for builders and that builders were good for Fianna Fáil. So now that Haughey had attained his goal and was thought to be the right man in the right place, going by his earlier career where he displayed his excellence in the Ministries of Justice and Finance. This would appear quite logical. When one also takes into account his patience, organisational ability, his expertise shown as shadow Minister for Health, his new image – off cigarettes and drink – and his attaining the highest post in the land after all the trauma he went through during the Arms Trial, one could feel that this man would be the man for the job. So people like Patrick Gallagher and Des Traynor set about rectifying Haughey's financial situation; Gallagher offering his own help and Traynor obtaining finances from various rich businessmen. The Allied Irish Bank, on of his biggest creditors, also helped by writing down Haughey's loans.

Now that Haughey was in power, his finances sorted out and the main problem identifies, one would think that he would be able to set about solving the problem. However, he seemed to be helpless and indecisive. Many people thought that the veto and limited loyalty that people like Colley and O'Malley were giving to Haughey should have been dealt with at an early stage and not allowed to fester and grow within the party. It would appear that Haughey was waiting to get his own mandate from the people before he could sort this out. He, however, did nothing about the economy. Plans to restrict the school bus service to rural school children and resource tax on farmers were quickly dropped and a 34% increase granted in the public service pay which increased the budget deficit by 50%, exacerbated the problem rather than set about correcting it.

Though he again referred to the 'living beyond our means' issue in the Ard Fheis address in February 1980, his main focus was the North. He declared that Northern Ireland had failed as 'a political entity' and that the whole question should be raised 'to a higher plane'. He stated that the Government's first priority to end partition and called on the British to declare " their interest in encouraging the unity of Ireland by agreement and peace", and he would seek the development of an "arrangement for which Irishmen . . . without a British presence but with . . . British goodwill will manage the affairs of the whole of Ireland in . . . partnership with the European Community". He later went to London to meet Prime Minister Thatcher. On the eve of this meeting Thatcher took the wind out of his sails by stating that the constitutional affairs of Northern Ireland were "for the people of Northern Ireland, this

Government, this (UK) Parliament and no one else". Haughey spent most of the time drawing a comparison of Ireland with the recent independence obtained from Britain by Rhodesia. After the meeting they issued a joint communiqué vouching "more regular meetings to achieve closer co-operation between our two countries", and that "any change in the constitutional status of Northern Ireland" would be with "the consent of the majority of the people of Northern Ireland".

Haughey set out to wage an international campaign to put diplomatic pressure on the UK to bring about a solution to the North. At this Irish-Americans were split on the methods of achieving a settlement. There were the politicians on one hand and the groups like Noraid, the A.O.H. and the Irish National Caucus, who supported the Provisionals. Sean Donlon, the Irish Ambassador, tried to cut out these militant bodies. Haughey wanted someone that could work with all the Irish-American groups and tried to shift Donlon to the U.N. Powerful Irish-Americans such as Speaker 'Tip' O'Neill, Senators Edward Kennedy and Daniel Moynahin and Governors Hugh Carey and Ronald Reagan opposed the move and Haughey backed down.

Haughey wanted to please the green belt of the party and put a lot of emphasis on the Northern question. It was not too long before it became a live subject when prisoners in the H-Block went on hunger strike to obtain political status. Then at a Bye-election campaign in Donegal, Síle De Valera criticised Margaret Thatcher's "lack of compassion" in dealing with the hunger strikers, much to the surprise of the Taoiseach, who was sharing the stage. He was livid at the timing of Síle's outburst as he was having delicate meetings on the North with Thatcher at that time, though he did not refer to it in his speech. A meeting of the two leaders took place a short time afterwards during an EEC summit meeting in Luxembourg where Haughey got no change out of the British Premier as she said she had nothing left to give, and anyhow, would not give, "concessions under duress". They met again in Dublin Castle where she was accompanied by Chancellor Geoffrey Howe and Foreign Secretary Lord Carrington, and the Taoiseach's party was Foreign Minister Brian Lenihan and Finance

Brian Lenihan, who held ministries in Justice, Education, Transport & Power, Fisheries and Foreign Affairs, Defence and Tánaiste.

Minister Michael O'Kennedy. Haughey may have felt that his reference at their first meeting to Carrington's solution to Rhodesia may have prompted Thatcher's decision to have included him in her party. Shortly after this meeting, Brian Lenihan told the author that he had great hope in Carrington, stating that he was above politics and would be able to look more objectively at the Northern question. The Ministers were excluded from the private meeting that Haughey had with Thatcher at the end of the day. After that meeting they issued a joint communiqué which described their talks as "extremely constructive and significant". Statements made afterwards by Haughey and Foreign Affairs Minister, Brian Lenihan, which hinted at changes in the constitution and an anticipated early end to partition were quickly contradicted by Thatcher. This led to a certain cooling of the relationships and led to intense Unionist opposition, spearheaded by Rev. Ian Paisley, the Democratic Unionist leader. This, and Haughey's and Lenihan's interpretations led to the calling off of the H-Block hunger strike. Haughey at this time received a lot of criticism from the opposition, particularly Labour leader Frank Cluskey and Fine Gael leader Garret Fitzgerald about the evasiveness of Haughey's answers to questions on the meeting, plus his decision to put the matter under confidentiality and secrecy.

Joint studies were then set up to study all aspects of the Northern situation. There was a suspicion that the security aspect of the studies included an Anglo-Irish defensive pact in return for ending partition. This was criticized by Garret Fitzgerald and Haughey did admit that if partition were ended, the Government would have to review ". . . appropriate defence arrangements for the island as a whole", and that the country would align completely with its European partners when the EEC became "a full political union".

Running side by side with the Northern problem was the economic scenario, which was spinning out of control, and Haughey seemed not to be able to control. In fact, many people believed he was not prepared to take the hard decisions he referred to in his 1980 Ard Fheis speech as he had planned an election and needed the populist support to achieve his own mandate. Haughey himself said that in view of the International recession a reduction in Government expenditure would lead to unemployment and hardship. To calls in the Dáil for cuts in expenditure, he retorted by stating that such a policy, "in our social and economic circumstances would be unrealistic and unacceptable". The figures at the time reflect how the financial situation deteriorated. A 1980 budget forecast an Exchequer Borrowing Requirement (EBR) of £896 million (v 1979 of £1,009) overshot to £1,217 million. The EBR for 1981 was set at £1,296 million, but by June it was estimated that it was so over budget that by the end of the year it would be £1,973 million (20% of GNP).

It would appear at this time, by his actions, that what he wanted was an election that would give him his own mandate and thus enable him to rid some of his most cumbersome Ministers, which would then enable him to get on with the job in hand. He still had in the Cabinet people who not alone were very much resentful of his leadership and were doing all in their power to get rid of him, such as Ministers, Colley and O'Malley, in particular,who it must be remembered were fellow architects of the Manifesto with Lynch and O'Donoghue. Colley at one time wanted a deal with Garret Fitzgerald re questions in the Dáil about the Arms Trial that could bring down the Government and possibly undermine Haughey's leadership, but Fitzgerald would not buy it, as Colley refused to give Fine Gael the appropriate motion on paper. At the same time, to ensure that he win the election, Haughey was not prepared to bring in the measures necessary to bring the Economy under control as this would not be a popular decision before the election. So, early in 1981, Haughey planned to go to the country after a successful, rallying Ard Fheis in February. But this was not to be as on the Friday night, St. Valentine's Day, forty-eight young people perished in a tragic fire in the Stardust night club in Haughey's own Constituency, and the remainder of the Ard Fheis, which would include the Taoiseach's address, was postponed until April. Other events such as the H-Block hunger strike, Bobby Sands, one of the hunger strikers, being elected as an M.P. to Westminster, and his death on May 5th, further hampered Haughey's plans and the election did not eventually take place until June 11th of that year.

The election campaign began well for Fianna Fáil showing 52% in the polls and were matching Fine Gael's proposed tax cuts with lavish spending plans for all the constituencies. The election was run in a Presidential manner with both leaders, Haughey and Fitzgerald, taking a tour around all the constituencies – Haughey by his son's helicopter, Fitzgerald by bus. Travelling by helicopter made it difficult for the press to keep up with Haughey and those that did became critical of the fact that he was answering all their questions with the same blasé general answers. Fitzgerald, on the other hand was the darling of the press, allowing them to travel in the bus with him and even asking their advice occasionally. As the campaign went on, the polls began to change for Fianna Fáil and the results of the election gave Fianna Fáil 78 seats out of 168. 45.3% of the poll was not enough to form a Government. Fine Gael and Labour took over the reins of Government with the help of the Worker's Party and an Independent, and Garret Fitzgerald became Taoiseach.

Immediately, the new Government embarked on corrective measures to bring the economy back in line; measures which led them to do a u-turn on their pre-election tax cutting promise. Haughey, now leader of the opposition, was vehemently opposed to this strategy of deflation and monetarism. Because of this he brought the ire of, not alone the Government, but some of the country's leading economists and a sizeable section within his own party. With regard to the economists he denounced Economics as a "dismal science". The leading critic in the party was Charley McGreevy, and this was surprising as he played a big part in the downfall of Lynch and the election of Haughey as leader. He may, however, have harboured a resentment against Haughey as he was not rewarded with even a Junior Ministry, while he saw all his colleagues who took part in the coup rewarded. He aired his views on his disagreement with Haughey's economic strategy in the *Sunday Tribune* and got the whip removed from him and he became an Independent T.D. This Coalition did not have a long life as they not only failed to implement the tax cuts they promised, but actually set about increasing taxation. The straw that broke the camel's back was Minister for Finance, John Bruton's attempt to put Value Added Tax (VAT) on children's shoes in the 1982 Budget. Independent Jim Kemmy, who had previously made his intention known regarding this tax, left the Coalition and the Government fell. As Garret Fitzgerald headed to Áras an Uachtarán to dissolve the Government, attempts were made by Fianna Fáil members to contact President Hillary to advise him not to dissolve the Government but to ask Haughey to try and form a Government, which is an option in our Constitution. These phone calls were to raise their heads in 1990 during the Presidential Election. In that year Brian Lenihan, who was a candidate, in an interview with Jim Duffy, a student doing confidential research for his thesis, said that he was one of the people who rang the President. It would appear that in his eagerness to point out that the President is above politics and if he was President he would not allow himself to be influenced by his former party, that he included himself as one of the callers. It should also be remembered that Brian Lenihan was under heavy medication at the time, having gone through a liver transplant earlier in the year. Garret Fitzgerald replaced another Fine Gael invitee on John Bowman's television current affairs programme, *Questions and Answers* to challenge Lenihan on whether he made the call or not. Lenihan denied that he had made the call on the programme, as he also did when questioned by Seán Duignan on the six o'clock news the next evening. In that interview he made the famous statement that "on mature recollection", he did not make the call. It probably lost the election for Lenihan as the polls favoured him up to then.

The election campaign saw differences of opinion on economic strategy between Haughey and his dissident Ministers – Colley, O'Malley and especially O'Donoghue, who contradicted Haughey on an RTÉ radio interview and avoided to answer a question on where he stood on Haughey as leader. The main thrust of Haughey's economic strategy was to rubbish the outgoing Coalition's Budget, though in the end, he decided to accept O'Donoghue's approach in terms of the current budget deficits and borrowing requirements, while eliminating the harsher elements of the Coalition's approach and adopting his own method of achieving it. The resulting election brought Fianna Fail back to power, with the help of Independent Tony Gregory and the Worker's Party, but not before a deal was struck up with Gregory and the Worker's party and a leadership challenge by Des O'Malley. A cabal of Colley, Seamus Brennan, former General Secretary and now newly elected T.D., Bobby Molloy, Jim Gibbons and Martin O'Donoghue decided to put Des O'Malley forward for leader at the next Parliamentary

Gerry Collins, who held ministries in Justice, Posts & Telegraphs and Foreign Affairs.

meeting. The media, especially the *Irish Independent* in the persons of Bruce Arnold and Raymond Smith, predicted that Haughey would be ousted 'as Jack Lynch had been' in 1979. Fianna Fáil dissidents felt that the 'Haughey factor' as they called it, cost the party an overall majority. This was endorsed, especially by recently returned Kilkenny Deputy, Jim Gibbons and outgoing Chairman of the parliamentary party, Waterford's Willie Kenneally, who had just lost his seat. Journalists Geraldine Kennedy and Sean Duignan called it right, and Albert Reynolds said that Haughey would easily win with the quip, "Who else would be able to deal with Tony Gregory and the Worker's Party?" The challenge failed miserably when at the quickly called parliamentary party, speakers Padraic Faulkner, Rory O'Hanlon, Jim Tunney and Liam Lawlor more or less asked O'Malley to back down and not split the party and to the surprise of his fellow plotters, Martin O'Donoghue, believing that the timing was wrong, called on O'Malley to withdraw his nomination in the interests of party unity. O'Malley duly withdrew his name. Many of the party accepted that only Haughey would have the ability to deal with Gregory. The deal which included nationalisation of land for Dublin docks and Clondalkin Paper Mills, finance for housing in inner Dublin and greater Dublin, and a job creation scheme over the next three years and extra remedial teachers for inner city. Though the deal came in for a lot of criticism, the need was there from neglect by various Governments over the years.

The new Government was stuck with the budget that Bruton had put in place, though Haughey insisted that the extent of the cut-backs in expenditure advocated by the Coalition was not necessary.

Haughey Back as Taoiseach After Eight Months

In the new Cabinet, Colley was not appointed Tánaiste due to his participation in the attempted heave against Haughey, nor did he continue to have a veto over the appointments to Cabinet of Ministers of Justice and Defence as he demanded in Haughey's first term as Taoiseach. After twenty years in Cabinet he returned to the backbenches as he refused other Ministries offered to him by Haughey. The Cabinet still had a mixture of factions. Ray McSharry was appointed Tánaiste, Albert Reynolds and Seán Doherty were given senior Ministries, while Tom McEllistrim, another of the 'Gang of Five', got a Junior Ministry. Dissidents O'Malley and O'Donoghue were also a the Cabinet table. Patrick Connelly became Attorney General.

At this time Jim Prior, the Secretary for Northern Ireland, was trying to introduce a devolved government in the North, and as Haughey believed that the system of governments of internal agreements had utterly failed, his first priority was to oppose this new initiative. Though Haughey and John Hume denounced the Secretary's remedy, Prior went ahead. This was to add to the deteriorating relationships between Haughey and Thatcher at this time. This was happening due to a number of factors on both sides; Thatcher was not happy that the Irish delegation at the summit in Dublin were trumpeting the advent of the end of partition and Ireland's refusal to adopt the EEC embargo on trading with Argentina, due to the Falklands war at the time, though they went along with the embargo at a later stage. Haughey was not happy with the British veto on an increase in farm prices. Haughey's reason for not supporting the embargo was due to the fact that "sanctions complimenting military action are not acceptable".

During this period a number of mishaps, some designed and some sheer coincidence, all contributed to an era which was described by long-time adversary of Haughey, Conor Cruise O'Brien, as the GUBU period. He concocted the slogan from Haughey's description of the arrest of murderer Malcolm McArthur in the apartment of the Attorney General, Patrick Connelly, which Haughey stated was grotesque, unbelievable, bizarre and unprecedented. All other misadventures at this time seem to then adopt the GUBU image. One of these was the offer by Haughey of the EU Commissionership to Fine Gael's Dick Burke, which would then create a Bye-election and give Fianna Fail a chance of winning an extra seat and strengthening their position in the Dáil. It backfired as Dick Burke accepted the EU job but Fianna Fáil failed to win the seat in west County Dublin, which went to an unknown Fine Gael candidate, Liam

Scally. Before the election Fianna Fáil had loosened up on their tight budgeting to soften the voter, but it did not work. Ray McSharry, Minister for Finance, now had to bring in a belt-tightening strategy of cut-backs and deferral of public pay increments. To add to Haughey's woes a further heave was set in motion against him when former ally Charley McCreevey put down a motion of 'no confidence' in the leader, and O'Malley, who disrupted a Spanish holiday

Charles Haughey at the Fianna Fáil Ard Fheis, 1986.

and O'Donoghue threw in their support. A major campaign in the form of McSharry, Reynolds and Doherty fielded for Haughey. This was ably assisted by phone calls by big contributors to the party to 'do the right thing' or else. A groundswell of grassroots also helped Haughey, as well as promises of promotions to some disgruntled backbenchers. On the day of the parliamentary meeting Haughey called for an open vote which he got by a vote of fifty-three to twenty-seven. This was followed by a vote on the motion which was won by Haughey, fifty-eight to twenty-two. Thus was formed what became as the gang of twenty-two.

The sudden death of Clare Deputy, Bill Loughnane and the hospitalisation of Jim Gibbons further reduced Fianna Fáil's majority in the Dáil, and when Tony Gregory and the Worker's party withdrew their support over the cuts, the Government fell on a vote of no confidence by Fine Gael by eighty-two votes to eighty. Other issues at the time which became part of the election campaign of the opposition were the performance of the Minister for Justice, Seán Doherty and the operation of the Garda force. Doherty, a former Garda detective, became involved in a number of controversies such as the Dowra affair, where a witness from the North was detained by the RUC and was not able to give evidence in a court case against Doherty's brother-in-law. Another incidence was the Tully affair in Roscommon where a Garda Sergeant successfully resisted a transfer in which the Minister was alleged to be involved.

The resultant election was a defeat for Fianna Fáil as they only won seventy-five seats with 45.2% of the vote, and Fine Gael and Labour formed a Government under Garret Fitzgerald. This Coalition lasted

The Taoiseach, Charles Haughey and his cabinet 1979.

until 1987. Shortly after the Coalition's assumption of power, the new Minister for Justice, Michael Noonan, announced that the former Fianna Fáil Justice Minister had organised the use of Garda equipment to tap the telephones of two journalists – Geraldine Kennedy and Bruce Arnold (*Irish Independent*) – and made a likewise arrangement to enable former Finance Minister Ray McSharry to bug a conversation he was having with Martin O'Donoghue, who indicated to McSharry that there were people willing to arrange finance to change the leadership of Fianna Fáil. This led to an Inquiry by the Parliamentary party into the allegations and the resignations from the Front bench of Doherty and McSharry. The outcome of the investigations was that sensitive information from Cabinet meetings was getting into the newspapers and that O'Donoghue had indeed offered to arrange financial help from certain areas to oust Haughey. The seriousness of the allegations led to a special meeting of the party on Sunday, 23rd January to discuss the implications of the revelations. Rumours were abounding about Haughey's impending resignation with stories of a number of T.D.s approaching him with advice to do so, combined with what looked like his political obituary in a feature on his life in the *Irish Press*. On the 27th of the month there was a general expectation that Haughey would resign at a parliamentary party meeting, but Haughey, with the moral support of Neil Blaney, P.J. Mara and Haughey's nephew, Seán O'Connor, said "We'll fight the c—ts.". At the parliamentary meeting Ray Burke stated that the leader should go when he decides to do so and Haughey agreed with this. The general thrust of the meeting was that it was only a matter of time before he would step down and Haughey survived again. Now that it seemed that a vacancy would exist for leader in the not too distant future, names of potential candidates began to sprout. The key contenders were Des O'Malley, Gerry Collins and Michael O'Kennedy. Brian Lenihan's and John Wilson's names also came into the reckoning. The next meeting of the parliamentary party was postponed at short notice due to the untimely death of Donegal Deputy, Clem Coughlin in a car crash. As the anti-Haughey faction, with stories of intimidating phone calls before the previous parliamentary meeting, were bent on putting the leadership question to a vote, they were angry that the opportunity had been so abruptly scuppered. They then demanded a special meeting for February 7th and this did look like the end for Haughey. However, Haughey did not contemplate defeat and attacked by stating that who should be the leader of Fianna Fáil should not be dictated by a "small rump within the party . . . the media or other people outside the party". He then sent a message out to all the Cumainn stating, "that its policies and its leaders in future should not be decided by the media, by alien influence, by political opponents or business people pursuing their own ends". He was further assisted by a demonstration of support outside Fianna Fáil headquarters where Niall Andrews made a passionate plea against the media, who he said were trying "to execute Haughey, just as the leaders of the 1916 rising had been executed". At the meeting Bertie Ahern read out the report of the parliamentary meeting on the phone tapping, which vindicated Haughey and put the blame more or less on Doherty. The seriousness of the phone tapping was lost in the even more serious cases of the fact that information leaking from Cabinet meetings could be seen as undermining the security of the State, and offers of financial assistance to elect or remove political leaders could be seen as undermining the very process of democracy. Though McSharry and Doherty resigned from the parliamentary party, Doherty was restored to the party in 1985 and McSharry returned to win an MEP seat for the party. The ensuing vote that took place saw Haughey still as leader by forty votes to thirty-three.

Haughey in Charge in Opposition

Haughey was now about to gain complete control of the party. As O'Donoghue and Jim Gibbons had lost their seats at the election and with the untimely death of George Colley in Guy's Hospital in London at the young age of fifty-seven, Des O'Malley was now a lone figure, as most of his other allies seemed to desert him. This allowed Haughey to now concentrate on being a strong opposition. Fitzgerald's attack on Fianna Fáil's appointees to the Planning Board by Ray Burke was met with strong opposition by Haughey. Fitzgerald and Spring, in a Fine Gael/Labour coalition set about changing the Planning Board's Directors to non-political appointees. Haughey retorted by stating that this was a most "Vindictive legislation" and withdrew the party from all Dáil Committees.

The next matter of contention was the New Ireland Forum in which there were differences of opinion on a United Ireland. Spring then accused Haughey of leaking information from the Forum and Haughey denied this to the extend of breaking down at the meeting and having to be helped from the meeting. In the end Haughey agreed to a final definition on a United Ireland of either it would be a unitary state, or a federal solution or a joint authority – "the political structure of political unity which the Forum would wish to see established". When the Forum's report was published in May 1984, Haughey reversed his position, saying that only a unitary state would bring peace to the North, much to the dismay of Fitzgerald, Spring and John Hume. This caused some disquiet in certain areas of Fianna Fáil as Haughey had taken that decision without consulting the parliamentary party. Senator Eoin Ryan called a meeting of the parliamentary party to discuss that issue, but at the meeting a majority of the members supported the Haughey line. However, Des O'Malley spoke out publicly about the "stifling of debate" within the party and had the whip removed from him by a vote of 56 – 16. This brought about the famous statement of Fianna Fáil Press Officer that there will be "no more nibbling at my Leader's bum", and the phrase that got him into hot water with his boss, 'Uno Duce, Uno Voce'.

Barry Desmond, Minister for Health in the Coalition Government brought forward legislation that would enable persons, other than married couples, to obtain contraceptives from chemist shops. Haughey opposed this as he said it would create "divisive debate" at a time when our people were subject "to grave economic and social issues". O'Malley disagreed with Haughey and said that the change was necessary "in the interest of the State, the Constitution and the

Republic". He then said he would stand by the Republic and refused to oppose the Bill. Haughey then called a meeting to expel O'Malley from the party, saying – "It's him or me". He appealed for a unanimous decision but had to be satisfied with an open roll call, which resulted in O'Malley being expelled by 73 votes to 9.

With O'Malley now gone from the party Haughey was in more control than he had ever been since he became Leader in 1979, and with Reynolds and Flynn on the Front Bench, there was now great confidence in the party of unseating a by now unpopular Coalition in the next election. The fact that there was no fight left in the anti-Haugheyites inside the party did not mean that things happening on the outside would not have a significant effect on the party at a later stage.

Shortly after O'Malley's expulsion, disillusioned Fine Gael member, Michael McDowell decided that if O'Malley wished to form a new party, he would be willing to join it. A poll carried out by Irish Marketing Surveys and organised by Seamus Brennan showed that 39% were in favour of a new party, as against 35% against. After a number of months and a number of meetings, with various people vacillating between joining a new party or not, the process was speeded up by the expulsion of Mary Harney from Fianna Fail after she publicly agreed with the Anglo-Irish Agreement, which had been strongly objected to by Haughey. She had a major influence in pushing O'Malley to start a new party. The Progressive Democrats were launched in Dublin on December 21st with Des O'Malley and Mary Harney being the first Deputies. Pierce Wyse was the next to follow and then later, which was a big surprise, was Bobby Molloy. Michael Keating, a Fine Gael deputy also joined. Other names associated with being about to join the new party – Seamus Brennan, Charlie McCreevy and David Andrews – decided to continue their careers with Fianna Fail. Michael O'Leary, who had lately resigned as Leader of the Labour Party, and had been elected as a Fine Gael deputy, was not accepted, as it might give the impression that the party was a refuge for misfits.

1986 was a bad year for the Fine Gael/Labour as the economy was going through a rough time with the National Debt going up and spending cuts beginning to bite. On top of that, the Coalition launched a Referendum on Divorce. Though Fianna Fail adopted a neutral stand on the issue, Haughey personally opposed it on the grounds, "that the importance of having the family as the basic unit of society", and that his "experience of life…" told him "…that there is a price to be paid for the introduction of divorce". 63% voted against it and the Referendum was defeated, which was another big blow to the Coalition Government. By the beginning of 1987, all was not well between the Coalition partners. Labour did not agree with the extent of the cuts that Fine Gael was introducing in the forthcoming budget and they left the Coalition on January 20th. Garret Fitzgerald asked President Hillary to dissolve the Government.

The election campaign began with Fianna Fail making no commitments, save a letter to the Irish Congress of Trade Unions that they would not have a policy of privatisation, Haughey stated that they would be seeking an Anglo Irish Agreement. Opinion polls in the early days showed Fianna Fail at 52%, Fine Gael 23%, Labour 5% and the Progressive Democrats 15%. Though the PDs were putting up candidates of the calibre of Geraldine Kennedy, Michael McDowell and ex-Fianna Fail members such as Anne Colley (daughter of the late George), Martin Gibbons and Pat O'Malley, it was Fine Gael they seemed to be affecting as their percentage wavered between 12% and 15%. All parties were attacking the PDs early in the campaign but they seemed to pull away from that tactic as the new party's prospects improved in the polls. When the election was over, the results were – Fianna Fail 81 seats; Fine Gael 51, PDs 14; Labour 12, Worker's Party 4 and Others 4. Though Haughey did not get his overall majority for the fourth time, he was sure he was going to be the next Taoiseach. The Progressive Democrats, though they prevented a Fianna Fail majority, did not achieve enough to remove Haughey from the chance of being Taoiseach. Ray Burke copper-fastened this by saying that they did not achieve this aim within the party and that they were not going to do it from outside it. Haughey also emphasised this. As Fianna Fail did not have to provide the Ceann Comhairle, and Sean Tracey of Labour showed an interest in the position, this left Fianna Fail with 81 votes for Taoiseach, and all the other parties, along with Jim Kenny, who stated he would not support Haughey, with 82. It was now up to Blaney and Gregory to elect the Taoiseach. Gregory abstained and Blaney voted with Haughey making it 82 – 82. The Ceann Comhairle, who had the casting vote, went in favour of Haughey, on the basis that only he had a chance of forming a Government.

Though throughout the previous years, and during the election campaign, Haughey had rejected the type of expenditure cuts that Fine Gael, in particular, had been advocating, once in power he proceeded not only to implement those very cuts proposed in the Fine Gael budget, but went beyond them. As everybody, including the dogs in the street, knew that the economy was in a bad state, he did not have much opposition to these stringent measures. He was helped immeasurably by the fact that on the night of the election results, Garrett Fitzgerald stated that he would not oppose measures taken by the new government to correct the economy.

Shortly after the defeat of Fine Gael, Fitzgerald stepped down as Leader of the party and, after a short election, Alan Dukes, with only six years Dail experience, defeated Peter Barry and John Bruton for the Leadership. He too, in what became known as the 'Tallaght Strategy', pledged to support Fianna Fail policies that would correct the economy.

Having the political will behind him, Haughey now circulated a letter to the senior Civil Servants in all departments seeking cutbacks from all of them for the remainder of 1987, 1988 and up to 1989. He said he wanted these reductions implemented by "the elimination of certain schemes and programmes ... overlaps and duplications between organisations ... mergers of organisations ... closure of institutions that had outlived their usefulness ... scaling down of operations of organisations and institutions ... and the disposal of assets which are no longer productively used". He also established an Expenditure Review Committee, which became known as 'An Bord Snip'. He was ably abetted in his strive for financial rectitude by Minister for Finance, Ray McSharry, who became known as 'Mac the Knife'.

Haughey's next step was to set up meetings with the Irish Congress of Trade Unions, employers, and the farmer's organisations in order to implement a new National Agreement for the next three years. His main aim was to get a national pay deal. He got along very well with al these bodies, much to the surprise and annoyance of the opposition, especially the Labour party. Others involved in the talks were Ray McSharry, Albert Reynolds and Secretary of the Department, Padraig Ó Huiginn, but the person who really made his mark (other than Haughey himself0 was the new Minister of Labour, Bertie Ahearn. The most amazing thing was that the Fianna Fail Government was able to negotiate amicably with the social partners in spite of the Government's cost cutting that was currently being pursued. The deal that they eventually came up with was the Programme for National Recovery, whereby the Unions agreed to a pay restraint of just 2.5% a year for three years and a deferral of special pay awards. This, together with the cuts in expenditure was the programme that paved the way for the Celtic Tiger of the 90s.

Haughey and the Great Economic Recovery

The economic recovery produced by the minority Haughey government of 87 was helped no doubt by the co-operation of Fine Gael under Alan Dukes, in what became known as the Tallaght Strategy – referring to a speech that Alan Dukes made in Tallaght – to the effect that they would support the Fianna Fail government if they introduced policies for economic recovery. Since Haughey had introduced the Fine Gael manifesto, and even went further, it made the job easy for Dukes. With the two parties now working hand-in-hand, it made the job easier for Haughey too. Any differences of opinion were usually worked out by the chief whips and the appropriate Ministers before they reached the floor of the Dail. This became frustrating for the Labour and PD parties and most of the opposition and trouble for Fianna Fail came from this area at a later stage.

A project of major significance at this stage that was more or less pushed through by Haughey was the International Financial Services Centre. The brainchild of NCB stockbroker, Dermot Desmond, it had been put on the long finger by the previous administration but was taken up by Haughey in opposition and followed through to fruition when he came to power. By 1999 it was giving employment to 11,000 people and contribution £1 billion to the Exchequer. The National Lottery was another bonus in that area as it produced a kind of saving that produced funding for many projects of benefit to communities that would otherwise have had to be funded out of the exchequer, or shelved.

Another area where Haughey changed his attitude was foreign policy. During his period in opposition he vehemently opposed the Anglo-Irish Agreement and was at loggerheads with the Department of Foreign Affairs at Iveagh House. He now began to work the Agreement, and due to the diplomacy of Foreign Affairs Minister, Brian Lenihan, patched up his differences with Iveagh House – though he still maintained control over Northern and European affairs in his own Department.

The first kink that came up for Haughey at this stage was the Extradition Bill. The major kidnapping of John O'Grady, nephew of Austin Darragh, seeking a ransom of £1.5 million and mutilation of his hand, together with the IRA bomb explosion which killed 13 people and injured hundreds of others, did not deter 57 deputies and senators, plus seven junior ministers from speaking against the Bill at a Fianna Fail parliamentary party meeting on November 18th. All were having problems with their own constituents. Haughey, however, came up with a formula that included safeguards whereby the Attorney General would vet all extradition applications. He eventually succeeded in getting the Bill into operation with relative ease.

The next issue in which the opposition were able to have a go at Haughey was the question of gifts being received from foreign dignitaries, after Haughey himself had been presented with a jewel encrusted dagger, and Mrs Haughey had obtained a valuable necklace. The government procedure instructions in dealing with such gifts was for "Ministers ... to accept ... inexpensive gifts and not to accept expensive gifts, or when presented return them", or that "any valuable gift should be the property of the State". Haughey refused to give any explanation to the Dail about the received gifts.

Another issue that came to light was the decision by Ray Burke, Minister for Energy and Communications, to establish the Independent Radio and Television Commission (IRTC) to monitor the introduction of commercial radio and television. Labour was worried about the ending of the State monopoly on broadcasting and there were also other concerns about the allocation of licences, particularly the allocation of the licence to Century Radio headed by a well-known Fianna Fail supporter.

Then came the beef controversy. At a press conference in June 1987 Haughey shared the stand with beef baron and friend, Larry Goodman, in launching a major promotion of the development of the beef industry. This was one of the biggest investment programmes ever for the food industry and included a £60 million input from the IDA and EEC, with £170 million coming in under Section 84 of the Finance Act. The first shots in the beef controversy came from Labour T.D., Barry Desmond, who stated in the Dail that £20 million of Export funds were being held up due to alleged fraudulent practices of the Goodman company being investigated by the Gardaí. He followed this up the next week by saying that the Department of Agriculture was imposing a fine of £1 million. Haughey defended Goodman and accused Desmond of attempting to sabotage the whole meat industry. Michael O'Kennedy, Minister of Agriculture, denied that his office had issued court proceedings against the Goodman organisation, but later admitted that irregularities of £7.5 million were notified to his Department. There were questions too as to the operation of state export insurance. Michael Noonan, Minister of Industry in the previous administration had suspended it and the Fianna Fail party had reintroduced it on resumption of power. There was concern that Goodman was getting more than a fair share of that insurance cover, plus the fact that the insurance was covering exports to Iraq, which was a risky country for exports at that time, together with the fact that there was £37 million more cover than there were meat exports.

Just as things seemed to be going well for the Haughey minority Government, Haughey returned from a successful visit to Japan to find that the Government was about to lose a vote on a private member's motion which was for an allocation of £400.000 to help haemophiliacs who had been infected with HIV from contaminated blood transfusions. Haughey was livid at the Government getting into this mess in his absence and said that if defeated, he would dissolve the Dail. The vote went against the Government and against the wishes of Ministers of the calibre of Reynolds, Flynn and Burke. Haughey duly called an election, the result of which was – Fianna Fail 77 seats (-4 seats) with 44% of the vote; Fine Gale 55 (+4); the PDs dropped from 14 seats to 6; Labour 16 seats; Worker's Party 7 seats, Greens 1 and others 4. As it was looking like stalemate, Haughey began talks with other party leaders and at the end of the discussions went into partnership with the PDs. Haughey was back as Taoiseach with his old adversary Des O'Malley as Tanaiste. This was an historic break as it was the first time for Fianna Fail to go into Coalition, and even more so that it was with the PDs – another masterstroke by Haughey. It was not accepted by all the party! Reynolds described it as "a temporary arrangement".

The Beginning of the End for Haughey

Now back in power, only with the blessing of the PDs, it was only going to be a short term reprieve for Haughey. The new term started with a high for Haughey, as it was Ireland's turn to have the Presidency of the EU, which would ensure that Haughey would be President, a post he would be delighted to fulfil.

As President, he did an excellent job, particularly with regard to the reunification of Germany, for which he received praise from German Premier, Helmut Kohl. The other presidential election, the Irish one, was not as successful for Haughey. Early in the spring, Dick Spring insisted that there should be an election for the president on this occasion, as there had been no presidential election since 1973, as all presidents since then had been candidates agreed to by all parties. With this in mind, Dick Spring got Mary Robinson, a former Labour senator to stand and she defeated Noel Brown, a nominee of other Labour deputies, for the Labour nomination. Fianna Fáil and Fine Gael did not nominate their candidates until much later in the year, which enabled Mary Robinson to tour the country and put herself in a very strong position for the presidency, before the others had been chosen. Brian Lenihen's name was mentioned early in the campaign but the party had reservations about the state of his health, as he had just received a liver transplant. Because of this, the selection did not take place until the autumn and he too had to go through a selection process, where he defeated Minister for the Marine, John Wilson, for the nomination by 51 votes to 19. Fine Gael did not have a selection process as they found it difficult to get a candidate and after a number of deputies, including Austin Curry, had refused the honour, Curry eventually saved the blushes of the faltering Fine Gael leader, Alan Dukes, and took up the gauntlet for the party.

Though Mary Robinson had established herself as a strong contender by now, Lenihan soon became the favourite. This was until a series of disasters befell him. On a Questions and Answers program on RTE1, he was quizzed by panellist Garrett Fitzgerald and a member of the studio audience, Brian Murphy, as to a phone call he was alleged to have made to President Patrick Hillary, asking him not to dissolve a government that Garrett Fitzgerald was about to dissolve in 1982, and requesting him to try and form a government under Charles Haughey. Brian Lenihan denied the allegation and though there were rumours that a tape existed confirming Lenihan's phone call, he denied the allegation again on the following night's news. Then, the script of the tape which had been done by student Jim Duffy for his thesis, clearly showed that

Lenihan had said to Duffy that he had made the phone call. It did not, however, prove that he made the call. As the question asked was research about a Presidential election, Lenihan may be trying to say to Duffy that, if he was elected he would be above politics and the Party or the Taoiseach, Haughey would not have any undue influence with him as was the case with Hillary. With the script from Duffy now out in the open and even played on the national airways, Lenihan still completely denied that the phone call happened. On the Six One news with Seán Duignan, using his famous legal expression 'on mature recollection' he reiterated that he did not make the call. Prior to this, Dukes, under pressure as leader of his own party, decided to shift the emphasis to Fianna Fáil by putting down a vote of no confidence on the Government to create a split in the coalition partners. Immediately, O'Malley rang Haughey and advised him not to commit the PDs in the vote of no confidence and then went off to a meeting in Europe. Further embarrassment ensued when Director of elections Bertie Ahern stated that Lenihan's proposed meeting with President Hillary, to clarify the 'phone call' episode, had been called off and Lenihan did not appear to be aware of the cancellation. This was followed by a number of meetings of O'Malley and Haughey, the outcome of which was O'Malley's request that Lenihan should resign to save the Government. The cabinet then met, without Lenihan and his sister, Mary O'Rourke, and the feeling was that Lenihan should go. Lenihan was then summoned to Haughey's residence in Kinsealy, where Haughey relayed to Lenihan, that the PDs were asking for his head and that he should resign. Lenihan said he would only resign if he lost the election. Haughey asked him to think about it. Later, as Haughey was at the airport meeting Queen Beatrix of the Netherlands, Lenihan, on a request from Haughey, met a number of senior ministers; Ahern, Flynn, Burke, Reynolds and chief whip Vincent Brady, who exerted pressure on Lenihan to resign and to cancel canvassing planned for Longford and Westmeath that day. At the airport, Haughey was denying that any pressure was on Lenihan to resign and that the decision to do so would be 'entirely a matter for my old friend'.

After lunch with Queen Beatrix, Haughey again met Lenihan at Leinster House and now presented him with a resignation letter to sign. Lenihan again refused, asked for more time to consider it and departed for Longford and Athlone, where he was met with a great reception and placards reading 'Don't Resign'. Though many phone calls and messages were coming from the Taoiseach's office, Lenihan's handlers refused to take them and that evening Lenihan decided that he was not going to resign and said so on RTÉ. Next morning, Ciarán Haughey's helicopter was circling Lenihan's house in Athlone which, together with a number of phone calls to his house, were endeavouring to bring Lenihan back for a meeting with the Taoiseach in Kinsealy, but the Lenihan's refused to answer and the helicopter landed back in Dublin.

Back in Dublin, Haughey had been advised by P.J. Mara and Charlie McCreevey to sack Lenihan. At a parliamentary party that morning there was lots of bad news for the party. Mary Robinson was way ahead of Lenihan in two polls, one of which, by IMS made the gap at 21%. Ahern said that a general election would see a big drop in Fianna Fáil's vote and Haughey stated it was now looking like an election. In the afternoon, the meeting was informed that Lenihan was turning up at 7pm for the vote of no confidence. Though Haughey wanted Lenihan's resignation to avoid an election there was fierce opposition to it from Paddy Power, M.J. Nolan and Ned O'Keeffe. On the recommendation of the Chairman, Jim Tunney that the decision be left to Haughey, the meeting ended without a vote. At 5.45pm Brian Lenihan rang Haughey, who asked him to resign. On Brian's refusal to do so, the Taoiseach sent a letter to the President to terminate Lenihan's ministry. It was formally done in the Dáil later by the Taoiseach, which induced a scathing attack on him by Labour leader Dick Spring which said Haughey was a 'virus' that created a 'cancer' in the 'body politic'. Though there were deputies that disagreed with Haughey's decision, they dutifully followed him through the lobbies to vote confidence in Haughey's government. After this, sympathy swung behind Lenihan in the presidential stakes, but it was too late and a scathing and ill-timed attack on Mary Robinson's 'new found interest' in her family by Padraig Flynn on a radio interview killed off any hopes that was left for a Lenihan success. Though Lenihan headed the poll in the first count with 44% of the vote to Robinson's 37% and Curry's 17%, the strength of Curry's transfers to Mary Robinson enabled her to became the first woman and the first non-Fianna Fáil backed president in the history of the state.

The Challenge for the Leadership

The sacking of Brian Lenihan, one could say, was the first major factor in the challenge for the leadership. The shift away from Haughey by Reynolds and Flynn, which had started with Fianna Fáil going into coalition with the PDs was now even more pronounced. Reynolds, who after that marriage, had described it as 'a temporary little arrangement' at a meeting in Cork had now, at another meeting in Cork, after the Presidential election, indicated that he would be a candidate in the leadership stakes 'if a vacancy arose'. At the parliamentary meeting to analyse what had gone wrong, only Liam Lawlor had the courage to tell Haughey that it was time for him to go. Haughey himself softened any criticism that might be coming at him by promising a commission that would study the party and by assuring the deputies that Fianna Fáil would be in power for another ten years. However, in the background, camps were hardening on both sides, with Geoghan-Quinn, Flynn, Michael Smith and Noel Tracey in the Reynolds corner and Burke, Ahern, Collins, Mary O'Rourke and ironically the recently sacked Lenihan in the Haughey camp. The paradox this time around was Haughey, like Jack Lynch, in the 70's, had grown aloof from his deputies, while the affable Reynolds, or, as that he had become known as 'Uncle Albert', like Haughey in his wilderness years, was always available to the backbenchers. In the meantime, Haughey, having got off lightly at the parliamentary meeting, decided to press on with economic strategy, putting together a programme for Government with the PDs. On the plus side, we had Ahern putting PESP Programme for government together, and progress was being made also in the legislation with regard to marital breakdown, decriminalisation of homosexuality and where condoms would be available to 17-year-olds. On the deficit side was a row by the government partners about the alleged malpractices in Goodman factories, which was settled with a compromise, whereby a judicial enquiry was set up to examine the meat industry as a whole. A spate of alleged scandals now followed, starting with the Greencore affair where Chris Comerford was forced to resign as Chief Executive over alleged irregularities in share options on a take-over deal. This was followed by the Telecom debate, whereby UPH a property company established by Haughey's friend, Dermot Desmond, bought property from Johnson, Mooney and O'Brien bakery and sold it on to another company who then sold it to Bord Telecom, whose chairman, Michael Smurfitt, turned out to have an interest in UPH. On advice from his close confidents Bertie Ahern, P.J. Mara, Padraig O'Huiginn and Seamus Brennan, Haughey decided to ask Michael Smurfitt and Seamus Parceir, Chairman of Custom House Docks Development Board, who also had an interest in UPH to step down from their respective chairmanships, on an RTE interview. This seemed to put things to rest, but he then stated that he would lead Fianna Fáil into the next general election and commented that 'some Chinese leaders go on into their 80's and 90's'. This was not taken lightly by some sections of the party. As rumours abounded again that Reynolds was going for the leadership, O'Rourke, John Wilson, Michael O'Kennedy, Gerry Collins and Ray Burke came out publicly in their support for Haughey. However, the challenge to Haughey's leadership came from, a surprise corner when four backbenchers, Noel Dempsey, Seán Power, Liam Fitzgerald and M.J. Nolan stated their concern with regard to the 'events' in the semi-state sector and how the Taoiseach handled it on the radio. Haughey called a meeting of the parliamentary party to quash this threat immediately. At the meeting on October 2nd, Power and Dempsey met the leader head-on, telling him that the people were 'disgusted' with the scandals and Haughey's relationships with . . . people at the centre of those alleged scandals. Other scandals were to follow. John Bruton stated that a confidential report done by Desmond's NPD for Aer Lingus subsidiary, Irish Helicopters, got into the hands of competitor, Celtic Helicopters, owned by Haughey's son, Ciarán. There was also questions asked as to how Haughey got an ESB pilot installation on his island, Innishvickillane. In anticipation of a rough time from the opposition on the Programme for Government, the danger of the Government falling, because of Michael McDowell's wish to break Fianna Fáil's 'scandals' and Albert Reynolds stubbornness not to give the PDs their way in the Programme for Government, was staved off by Bertie Ahern. In a meeting with Reynolds, Bobby Molloy and Des O'Malley, he convinced them to let go of their various differences and push ahead with the Programme for Government, for which Haughey praised him by saying 'He's the best, most skilful, most devious and most cunning of them all'. The key to the Fianna Fáil agreement on the Programme for Government was Fianna Fáil giving in to the PDs request to reduce personal taxes from 33% to 25% by 1993 in preference to Fianna Fáil's own trust in the programme of social spending. In November 1991 more stories of alleged scandals broke. More irregularities in the Goodman organization were coming up in evidence at the meat tribunal and it became public that another friend of Haughey's, Pino Harris, had made a profit of £1.5 million on a deal whereby University College purchased Carysfort College out of the exchequer funds. These and the relationship between Haughey and Greencore chairman Bertie Cahill brought stern attacks in the Dáil from opposition leaders John Bruton and Dick Spring. A parliamentary party meeting brought a row between acting chairman Brian Lenihan and Charlie McCreevey, where the latter, who had publicly requested a vote of no confidence on the leader, wanted the question of the scandals cleared up. Some of the younger TDs were upset with Lenihan, who advised them that if they wished to discuss the leadership, it should be put on the agenda. After the meeting ended, Seán Power handed in a vote of no confidence in Haughey into the whip's office. This sudden action had taken Reynolds by surprise, but he took the bull by the horns and in a statement in the following Saturday said, "The well-being of our country requires strong and decisive leadership of government and of the Fianna Fáil party. I am not satisfied that that leadership now exists. I will be supporting the motion . . ." Within one hour, Haughey sacked him. The same treatment was meted out to Flynn, Geoghan-Quinn, Smith and Treacy, who came out in support of Reynolds. Haughey was now publicly supported by Ahern, O'Rourke, Burke, and Collins, who did so on RTE1 with the now famous appeal in tears not to 'bust up the party'. At the parliamentary party of 7th November that lasted fourteen and a half hours, Haughey got off to a good start when he won the opening round to have an open vote by 44 votes to 33. Reynolds accused Haughey's people of a smear campaign against him, that there was surveillance carried out on his house and apartment. A number of Reynolds supporters made their case, the strongest coming from Padraig Flynn who using the third party 'Pee Flynn' stated that the leader was responsible for all the problems, for bringing the party into coalition and that 'Pee Flynn would be doing himself an injustice if he did not support the motion to discontinue the leadership forthwith of Charles J. Haughey.' The motion was defeated by 55 votes to 22 and Charles Haughey had survived again, but this time for not long more. This victory again gave Haughey a new belief in himself, but it was only a false sense of security. In his ensuing cabinet reshuffle, by choosing backbenchers Jim McDaid and Noel Davern for the two senior cabinet positions, he leapfrogged some junior Ministers who he had promised promotions to in the heat of battle and now neglected to acknowledge them in the rewards. The immediate problem he had was that Fine Gael and the Worker's Party soon brought to the Dáil, the fact that McDaid, the new Defence Minister, had been a witness for an IRA activist, James Pius Clarke, in an anti-extradition case and was photographed with him afterwards on the steps of the court. In view of the sensitivity of the Ministry, Des O'Malley called an urgent meeting with Haughey. The appointment of McDaid was delayed and, to avoid a circus, he withdrew his name from consideration.

The final nail in Haughey's coffin came however from an interview by former Justice Minister, Seán Doherty, on a late-night entertainment programme on RTE Network 2 called *Nighthawks*, in which he stated that others in Cabinet knew that he was involved in phone tapping the phones of Geraldine Kennedy and Bruce Arnold, when he was Minister for Justice in 1982. Other Ministers of that Cabinet, including Des O'Malley, said that the phone-tapping issue was never discussed at Cabinet, so the question was then – who else knew? This was finally answered by Doherty six days later at a press conference in the Montrose

Hotel when he stated that the then Taoiseach, Charlie Haughey, not only knew but that he had personally handed transcripts of the telephone conversations which he had received from the Deputy Garda Commissioner, Joe Ainsworth to Haughey. After Des O'Malley listened to a tape-recording of these admissions he knew that they could not stay in Government. The next day they did not attend a Cabinet meeting. Though Haughey in a press conference denied he knew about the phone-tapping, that his story was consistent and that Doherty's was not, the writing was on the wall. He further tried to say that this issue was a plot by the 'Country and Western Alliance', i.e. Flynn, Geoghan-Quinn and Reynolds, etc. against him. This did not wear however with the P.D.s, and they intimated that their price for continuation with Fianna Fáil in Government was Haughey's head. Haughey then had a meeting with Tánaiste John Wilson and Bertie Ahern, and to avoid a General Election Haughey agreed to stop down, providing that the P.D.s would give him breathing space to "depart with dignity". On January 30th, he informed the Fianna Fáil parliamentary party that he was resigning. On February 11th he resigned as Taoiseach and finished up by stating, "The work of Government and of the Dáil must always be directed to the progress of the nation, and I hope that I have been able to provide some leadership to that end in my time. I have always sought to act solely and exclusively in the best interest of the Irish people. Let me quote *Othello*, 'I have done the state some service; they know't. No more of that;".

The succession stakes began immediately with Albert Reynolds throwing his hat into the ring, being backed by Michael Smith, Máire Geoghegan-Quinn, David Andrews, Seamus Brennan, Tom Kitt, Ben Briscoe, Charlie McCreevey and Brian Cowen. Ahern was expected to follow suit, and was backed by pro-Haughey deputies like Gerry Collins, Brian Lenihan, Rory O'Hanlon and Ray Burke. Reynolds, who was the exciting risk-taker who signified change, was favoured by the younger deputies looking for promotion versus the more conservative Haugheyites, who chose more of the same. Ahern, feared that if things went the wrong way, his future prospects might be damaged or at least delayed. In addition, comments made public by Smith about Ahern's unclear marriage situation and Reynolds' comments that "People do like to know where the Taoiseach of the day is living", probably made up Ahern's mind that

Máire Geoghegan-Quinn, held ministries in The Gaeltacht, Justice and Communicatins.

the timing was not right. He had a meeting with Reynolds and decided not to go forward on the promise that he would be promoted to number two and thus be the heir apparent. His backers were furious. Two others entered the fray, but in the ensuing election at the parliamentary party meeting on February 6th, Reynolds achieved 61 votes to Michael Woods' 10, and Mary O'Rourke's 6. On February 11th he was appointed Taoiseach with the backing of his 'temporary little arrangement' partners – the P.D.s. His first job as the Taoiseach was the selection of his cabinet, where he sacked eight Ministers, including Burke, O'Rourke and Collins. He returned Flynn, Geoghan-Quinn and Smith to Cabinet, promoting McCreevey, David Andrews, Brian Cowen and Noel Dempsey. He also sacked some junior ministers who would be loyal Haugheyites, like Dermot Ahern and John O'Donohue.

Albert Reynolds – The Taoiseach from Longford

Albert Martin Reynolds was born in the village of Rooskey on November 3rd, 1932, the youngest of four children of John P. and Catherine Reynolds. The family, consisting of brothers Jim and Joe, and sister Teresa, lived on Main Street, Rooskey, where John P. ran the business of farming, coach building and undertaking. The coach building shed later became a dance hall. Albert attended the national school in Rooskey but later changed to the national school in Carragine, a one-teacher school four miles from Rooskey run by Elizabeth McLoughlin, which had a reputation for achieving scholarships. Rightly enough, Albert won a scholarship to Summerhill College, a boarding/day school in Sligo, the only member of his family to go to secondary school. His early friends in Rooskey were the Cashins, Cronins and Hanleys, of which Peter

Albert Reynolds, former Taoiseach, Minister for Finance, Minister for Industry and Commerce and Minister for Posts and Telegraphs.

Hanley, later of Hanley's Meats, Rooskey, was to be a lifelong friend. In an RTÉ radio interview on a series of programmes on former Taoisigh in 2001, Reynolds described his time in Summerhill as a place where "you got away from it all. It made you very independent. You had to make do with what you had – you had to sort out your resources no matter how limited they were – you had to improvise".

And at improvising he excelled. He would bulk-buy sweets and sell them at a profit. His expertise in this area came to the notice of the authorities and he was put in charge of the tuck shop, the profits of which were ploughed back into better sporting facilities for the students. Both teachers and fellow students at Summerhill described Reynolds as being 'a good mixer and a very practical fellow, able to talk to anybody and everybody's friend', 'bright eyed and bushy tailed', exceptional student of the Classics', and 'friendly with everybody'. His extra-curricular activities were rugby, table tennis, snooker, billiards and dancing. The latter was to play a significant part in his later life. His earlier ambitions to become a teacher were scuppered when he broke a leg during the

Leaving Certificate exam in 1952. He did however attain his Leaving Certificate with honours in Irish, English and Classics.

His first job was with J.C. McLoughlin's hardware, Pearse Street, Dublin, at a wage of £2 10s a week. While there, the manager, Mr Taylor, gave Reynolds some advice that he was to remember for the rest of his career, which was – "If you don't think where you are going, you'll be licking stamps for the rest of your life. It is not a question of being someone, but rather choosing to do something, and doing it better than anyone else". His next job was as a cabinet polisher for the Pye Radio factory in Dundrum, also taking up a night course in accountancy. In addition, he did the exams for Bord na Móna and C.I.É. This led to his next job as a clerk for Bord na Móna in Ballydermot in Offaly for £3 10s a week, subsidised by renting a plot of turf which was a custom there of Bord na Móna with the locals, and making an extra cash for himself each week. His next job with C.I.É. brought him to Dromod, Co. Leitrim, practically down the road from his home, where he increased his weekly wage by £1. It was here he was to meet Kathleen Coen; they fell in love and married in the early '60s. It was during this period that he got involved in a business that was to have a significant part in his life. As secretary of the Rooskey Carnival local church collection fund, in 1955 he was responsible for booking the bands and marquee. This was a huge success, paying off the church debt in two years. Albert and his brother Joe decided to keep the carnival business going, continuing the success for a further two years. At this time, Albert's brother Jim came back from Australia and he joined Albert in another business, running dances. Albert still worked for C.I.É. by day. The dance business became so lucrative that he had to make a choice between C.I.É. and running dances when his manager decided to transfer him to Wexford. The market was just coming right at the time, as it was the beginning of the era of the 'Ballrooms of Romance' and the great Showbands like the Clipper Carlton, the Royal Showband with Brendan Boyer, the Miami, with Dickie Rock, Brendan O'Brien and the Dixielanders, and many more. It was a time of change in Ireland with Lemass' First Economic plan and more disposable income from the many factories springing up as a result of that plan. Jim invested £5,000 to build their first Ballroom in Rooskey and they called it *Cloudland*. Jim, who had made his money in construction in Australia, concentrated on the building, while Albert looked after booking the bands and collecting the money. This was to be the beginning of a chain of fourteen ballrooms stretching from Strabane to Limerick and from Roscommon to Wexford, as well as renting other halls.

The end of the 60s saw the decline of the showband era. International acclaim, higher fees, shorter hours on the stage and the fact that Ballrooms could not get drink licences all combined to drive the clients to the pubs where they could enjoy the new phenomena of Cabaret. The younger set were being attracted to the Disco scene. The rise in Country and Western and Bingo were also factors. Albert Reynolds had already spotted this trend towards Bingo and was one of the first in the country to adapt to it, bringing in prizes of £1,000. After a serious business difference with his brother Jim, Albert decided in 1966 to get out of the ballroom business altogether. Reynolds also had an interest in two profitable property companies – J.P. Reynolds Ltd. and Land Ltd., set up with his brother in 1994.

Albert's next venture was the building of a swimming pool for the town of Longford. A company – The Longford Development Company – was set up for the purpose whose directors were Albert Reynolds, Mattie Lyons, Dessie Hynes, Frank Carter T.D. and Larry Donegan. It was a major project for its time and was financed 50% by the Department of Local Government under Minister Neil Blaney, 1d/£ rates by Longford County Council, and funds raised by carnivals and dances by the Longford Development Company. The latter was an area where Reynolds had lots of experience and contacts. The completed swimming pool, which cost £16,000, was handed over to Longford County Council on October 17th, 1969.

This project completed, Reynolds purchased Paddy Kehoe's meat company in Francis Street in the Liberties in Dublin. This had originally been the old Kehoe-Donnelly's factory and was now losing money hand over fist, but Reynolds running the show in pig killing and curing, mostly for export, turned it into a profitable company in one year and sold it off in 1973.

His business took another direction when he purchased a pub in Malahide for £33,000 and turned it into a Cabaret centre which was the then up and coming thing and was again being a 'hands on' man, dishing out pints of porter. It was however burned to the ground on one stormy night, but he was covered by insurance to the tune of £83,000. He then turned his hand to the fish exporting business, Donegal being his main source of supply. A major cartel, including Billingsgate of London, ganged up on him, leaving with £100,000 of unmarketable fish on his hands. He had to keep cool and think fast, as fish is a most perishable product. He put it all into refrigeration, held it till Christmas and sold it off for smoking. He came out of it alright. After a stint at a not too successful Finance company, ABC Finance, he acquired a local newspaper, *The Longford News*, and a share in the Odeon Cinema.

Reynolds Ventures into Petfoods

While running the meat business in the Liberties, the notion came to Reynolds of setting up a petfood company. He discovered that the people that he was paying to take away the offal from the factory were freezing it and selling it to companies in the UK who were using it to manufacture pet food. However, when he decided to build a factory in Longford for processing pet foods – C & D Petfood Ltd. – people thought he was mad. Again Albert Reynolds' timing was perfect, as pet food was beginning to take off in the supermarkets. The total market for petfoods in Ireland at the time was £7 million and it was mostly supplied by British suppliers. The UK market itself was £240 million. At the same time as Reynolds was throwing the idea of a pet food business around, his friend Mattie Lyons was thinking along similar lines as his factories, Lyons Meats in Longford and Dromad, had been supplying offal to Scottish businessman, John Hammond for some time. In fact, Lyons had discussed the idea of a petfood factory with Hammond. It was however, after he discussed it with Reynolds and Dublin publican, Dessie Hynes that the idea took root. A company, Canine Foods Ltd. was set up with the following shareholders: - Mattie Lyons (51%), Reynolds (29%), Arthur McManus, a Dublin businessman (10%) and John McShane, who had experience in meat canning and petfoods, the remaining 10%. Due to a clash of names with a UK company, the company name was changed to C & D Petfoods Limited, later again changed to C & D Foods Ltd. A site was acquired by Mattie Lyons for £600 in Edgeworthstown. The project was grant aided by the I.D.A, and finance by the AIB, the I.C.C. and the shareholders. The factory was officially launched on July 1st, 1971 in Dublin. Initially it encountered major problems. Two marketing experts from the UK – Bruce Spence and Thomas Woodcock of Statmead Marketing Company – were brought in to help. This company had a van sales force in the UK specialising in sales of wine and pet foods. Following meetings between Statmead, Córas Trachtála and various buyers, it was agreed that Reynolds and Lyons would get 5% of Statmead, while Spence and Woodcock would receive 25% of the profits of C & D, together with 10% of the sales of that company. After a number of product and personnel failures, getting only 50% of the original grant promised by the IDA and near liquidation, a new general manager, Mervyn Mudd was brought in with a package that included 5% of the company shares. After this the fortunes of the company picked up and orders were obtained in Italy, the UK and Denmark, the most important of these being a £200,000 order for own-brand petfoods from Sainsbury's, one of the UK's most prestigious supermarket chains, and it being own brand, saved the expense of advertising. Dividends obtained by Reynolds to the order of £90,000 in the years 1974-76 would mean the company was making money. A dispute between Reynolds and Lyons ended up in the High Court and though Justice Kenny found in favour of Lyons, he ordered Lyons to sell his shares to Reynolds. The factory still operates today, where it is still one of the main employers in Edgeworthstown.

The Longford News

Vincent Gill, an eccentric character, ran *The Longford News* for many years and towards the end of his life he did not want it to fall into the hands of his competitor, *The Longford Leader*, who would probably buy it and close it down. He offered it to local businessman Dessie Hynes, who in turn offered it to Albert Reynolds, who purchased it for £12,000. As Albert was too busy to operate it himself, he brought in Derek Cobbe to run it for him as editor and Eugene McGee. Albert allowed the editor to run it as he wished and did not try to impose his own influence or politics on it. The paper expanded quickly under Cobbe and it was sold in 1980 to *The Meath Chronicle* for £100,000. Cobbe purchased it back again in 1983, reselling it to *The Leitrim Observer* in 1990. It was later sold on to *The Roscommon Champion*.

Coalition of Fianna Fáil Collapse

The ironic thing about Albert Reynolds becoming leader of Fianna Fáil and Taoiseach is that it was helped by the P.D.s pulling the plug on Charlie Haughey, and in spite of Reynolds' earlier quip that their relation in Government was only "a temporary little arrangement". The question was, how long would it last? In the aftermath of the X Case, and the ensuing Referendum, strains crept into the relationship, with Fianna Fáil taking the conservative Pro-Life road and the P.D.s taking the more liberal route of Pro-Choice. However, the P.D.s pulled back from making it an issue that would bring down the Government. Throughout the year 1992 the polls were reflected a high 50% for Fianna Fáil and 4% for the P.D.s. another great asset Reynolds had was the good personal relationship which he had with British Prime Minister, John Major, a relationship they developed when Reynolds was Minister for Finance and Major was Chancellor of the Exchequer. Reynolds was only Taoiseach for a fortnight when Major invited him to the UK. This relationship was invaluable to Reynolds when he embarked on his Northern Peace Process, However, his impetuousness, led no doubt by the polls, caused Reynolds to declare at the Ard Fheis in March that, "Fianna Fáil did not need another party . . . as its conscience". This unnecessary remark was added to by Brian Cowen's warm-up speech before Reynolds' address when he asked the question, "What about the P.D.s? . . . When in doubt, leave out". This was the beginning of the rift that led to the break-up of the Coalition. The Tribunal of enquiry into the Beef Industry did the rest.

The Beef Tribunal came about by the introduction and implementation of the beef export credit, which was a system of guarantee of pay-up by the State in the event of default of payment by the country being exported to, which in this case was Iraq. This export credit was withdrawn by the Fine Gael/Labour Coalition on the basis that it was too risky due to the Iran-Iraqi war. When Fianna Fáil returned to power in 1987 they re-introduced it and a multi-million pound insurance cover was given to the Goodman Company by Reynolds, who was then Minister for Industry & Commerce. A number of factors soon came to be the cause of some concern to Des O'Malley, leader of the P.D.s and Tánaiste, and Labour leader Dick Spring and other Labour Deputies. These included (a), the fact that the insurance cover had risen to £250 million; (b) that 38% of the 'export sales' of Irish beef were in fact beef imported from Britain and Northern Ireland and re-exported; (c) that the Goodman group were getting the bulk of the cover, and (d) a BBC *World in Action* programme exposed irregularities and malpractices in the beef industry in Ireland.

As well as that, Reynolds had a suspicion that the P.D.s were out to get him and would use the Tribunal vehicle to do so. The P.D.s, on the other hand, felt that Reynolds and the Fianna Fáil party would orchestrate issues to undermine them and that other important matters were being kept from their leader. In June, O'Malley was called as a witness for the Beef Tribunal and this was watched carefully by all, as he had stated while in opposition and indeed, made a written submission to the Tribunal that Reynolds, while Minister for Industry& Commerce had favoured Goodman with the export credit scheme. Then, during the Tribunal he attacked the Taoiseach of having made decisions when in Industry & Commerce that were – "wrong . . . grossly unwise, reckless and foolish". Reynolds was called to give evidence in the autumn. He stated that he ran his department with the minimum of bureaucracy, in fact all he needed was the information on "one sheet of paper", and if he required more he knew where to get it. He was immediately called 'The one page man' by the media. When cross-examined by Adrian Hardiman, O'Malley's council, on the issue of export credit and in spite of advice for caution from his senior civil servants and political advisors, he went to describe O'Malley's evidence as "reckless, irresponsible and dishonest". The word 'dishonest' spelt the death knell to the Coalition and a few days later they, (the P.D.s) said they would favour a motion of 'no confidence' in a government of which they were a part, a motion that was then put down by Fine Gael and the Government was dissolved on November 5th.

It was difficult now to see how Fianna Fáil would get back in Government without achieving an overall majority. With the acrimonious break-up of the Fianna Fáil/P.D. coalition, there seemed to be no chance of that partnership getting together again. Labour leader, Dick Spring, seemed to rule out any chance of a Fianna Fáil/Labour alliance. He stated that he would not get "involved in a government that would bring politics into disrepute, like this one. He attacked Reynolds as a Taoiseach who promised "respect for the institutions of the house . . and lost . . . that he had promised open government but fought in the High Court for Cabinet confidentiality . . . who promised 'consensus' but . . . "governed behind closed doors". To add further to Reynolds' woes many of his own T. D.s and Ministers dodged going on TV or Radio to defend the Government's performance. In addition, the Pro-Haugheyites were smiling at Reynolds demise which threatened to make him the shortest reigning Taoiseach in the history of Fianna Fáil. The Fine Gael leader, John Bruton, entered the hustings with the idea of a Rainbow Coalition which included all other parties other than Fianna Fáil and Democratic Left. Dick Spring was livid that he had not consulted with him on this proposition. In fact, Bruton had spun this idea without consulting his own party. Spring, who really excelled in the Dáil prior to the election was now experiencing a big swing to his party which prompted him to propose a situation that if he were to go into coalition with any other party he would be looking for his turn as Taoiseach – in other words a 'rotating Taoiseach'. Reynolds on the other hand had dropped twenty points in the polls. When the votes were counted however, a hung Dáil was all that could be seen. Fianna Fáil had dropped ten seats which brought them below the 40%, the lowest they had achieved since 1927. Fine Gael also dropped ten seats and Dick Spring and Labour had an increase of seventeen seats, bringing them up to thirty-three. Though Reynolds initially took the result very badly, when he saw that nobody had a clear majority he soon felt that there was a possibility of a Fianna Fáil/Labour pact. To add hope to that, Brian Lenihan, who had a good cross-party image, advocated Fianna Fáil/Labour alliance as the most likely bet. Though the writing at times seemed to be on the wall for Reynolds as Taoiseach, failure by the so-called Rainbow Coalition to come to an agreement and the fact that Reynolds had come back from an EU Summit where he had achieved £8 billion in European Structural & Cohesion funds, enabled him to play the waiting game and eventually entice Dick Spring and Labour into a New Coalition with Albert as Taoiseach and Spring as Tánaiste and Minister for Foreign Affairs. He had said to Seán Duignan "Eight billion, Diggy, eight billion. Tell that to the begrudgers. Now watch me put a government together".

On arrival back from the Summit, Reynolds, accompanied by Seán Duignan, met Spring and Fergus Finlay and the two leaders retired to a private room and had a meeting that lasted about an hour. Reynolds then left and Spring went to meet his Labour colleagues in another room. This contingent was made up of Barry Desmond, Ruarí Quinn, Brendan Howlin, Pat Magnier, James Wynne and Fergus Finlay, together with economic advisors Willie Scally and Greg Sparks. Spring's brother Donal and John Rogers were also present. Spring told the meeting that Reynolds was willing to do business and that he had a better briefing than the P.D.s had got before they entered coalition with Fianna Fáil. To the question of the Beef Tribunal being a possible 'time bomb', he said that at the worst, Reynolds would be reprimanded for carelessness or incompetence. Though Quinn and Howlin were in favour of a Fianna Fáil/ Labour pact, Desmond and Finlay were for an option of a Rainbow Coalition plus the P.D.s. On a vote, five voted for coalition with Fianna Fáil, five were in favour of a Rainbow with the P.D.s. and Democratic Left. As Bruton would not have any truck with Democratic Left, the result was becoming inevitable. The next day the Dáil met but failed to elect a Taoiseach. Shortly after this the Labour parliamentary party met to give Spring a mandate to open negotiations with Fianna Fáil. Formal negotiations started on December 16th. The Fianna Fáil team was made up of Ahearne, Dempsey and Cowan, whilst the Labour team was Quinn, Howlin and Mervyn-Taylor. The discussions were open and frank with information from all Departments, including Finance, being made readily available to Labour.

The Ins and Outs of the Fianna Fáil – Labour Coalition

The initial distrust that was there between the two parties based on a certain section of the Labour party, especially of the Fergus Finlay ilk, and the further differences caused by the Labour Programme Managers, was no doubt going to be put under more strain by the upcoming Beef Tribunal report. Fianna Fáil would have its own problems with former prominent Ministers like Ray Burke and Gerry Collins, together with newer former Ministers like John O'Donoghue and Dermot Ahearne lurking and planning in the back benches with their Leader-in-waiting, Bertie Ahern.

In the meantime, Reynolds was turning his attention to the North, an area that was to be the shining performance of his Taoiseachship. From 1999 onwards John Hume had defied all critics and started a peace initiative with Gerry Adams. This involved a process of peace based on self-determination for the North. In 1991, Charlie Haughey and John Major were putting forward a motion of Joint Declaration between the UK and Ireland that would end violence by bringing republicans into mainstream politics.

When these propositions were eventually put to John Major he rejected them out of hand as they included as its object a United Ireland. Reynolds, when he came to power, picked up the pieces and began to build an initiative which would bring nationalists into the political arena and he invited Ulster Unionists to negotiate with the Dublin Government for the first time in Dublin. This process was aimed at bringing all the parties into a peace path and including them in the make up of the future political structure of the island of Ireland.

Seán Duignan, in his book *One Spin on the Merry-go-Round*, says that Reynolds informed him that he was in the process of convincing the Republicans the benefits of democratic politics rather than the armed struggle, and that they should not put a time-scale on a united Ireland, rather to accept that it would be by consent and on the self-determination of all the people of Ireland. When asked if he had told Spring about this he said he had and that Spring said, "You are on your own, Albert".

From 1989 onwards, Gerry Adams and John Hume had been having talks and in 1991 had presented a document from these talks to the Irish Government. Though Major did not want to accept these papers on the basis of the fact that he was being asked to be the persuader for a United Ireland, Reynolds however sent the papers to Major with the promise that it would bring about a cessation of violence and bring Republicans to the idea of an accepted consent and self-determination for the people of Northern Ireland.

Ironically, the process appeared to be speeded up by two violent acts – the killing of ten Protestants by an IRA bomb on the Shankill, and a retaliatory killing of a number of Catholics in the Greysteel pub by Loyalist Paramilitaries. This in an odd way may have spurred the two sovereign Governments to act. Reynolds invited Major to a Summit in Dublin. This led to a number of heated debates between Reynolds and Major, both in front of their respective delegations and in private. This Summit meeting paved the way for the signing of the Joint Declaration in Downing Street on the following week December 13th, 1993, in the very room where Michael Collins and Arthur Griffith signed the treaty in 1922. This was a truly historic occasion and was to eventually lead to the IRA ceasefire and the Good Friday Agreement. Around this time a number of issues began to raise their ugly heads which would lead to a deterioration of the ever-sensitive relationship between Reynolds and Spring. Spring, as the Labour leader was very aware that there were a sizeable number within his ranks who disagreed with the Labour/Fianna Fáil Coalition and to prove to them that he had done the right thing he not alone wanted to show that the Programme for Government was being implemented but that they as a party were getting their equal recognition for it. Reynolds, on the other hand, thought that Spring, ably helped by Findlay's media PR campaign, was trying to dominate the coalition. In early 1993, an attempt by Reynolds to sell of 25% of Telecom to Cable & Wireless was strongly opposed by Spring, who insisted that no State assets be sold during the life of the Coalition. Reynolds reluctantly backed down.

A second Tax Amnesty, proposed by Fianna Fáil, was opposed by a number of Labour Ministers and Spring, thinking that both Minister for Finance, Ahern and a number of Fianna Fáil Cabinet colleagues were against it and would thus talk Reynolds out of it. However, at the Cabinet table Ahern was for it, and to Spring's surprise and annoyance it went through. Another measure that Reynolds was trying to get through the Finance Bill was a measure that would give the Irish 'Super Rich' less rigid residency requirements for tax purposes. Spring faxed Reynolds, who was on holidays abroad, a warning that he would not agree with this. Reynolds was furious and contacted Ahern who dashed to Tralee to have a meeting on the issue with Spring. Eventually Reynolds backed down and went instead for a watered-down version of the measure. As relationships got worse the Coalition was hit with the 'Passports for Sale' dilemma. This was a method of offering citizenship to non-nationals for a cash investment. It was discovered that the Reynolds' family business had benefited from this system to the tune of £1 million.

Spring however, having inspected the files, came to the conclusion that everything was 'above board' and for his pains was described by the PD's Michael McDowell as being "morally brain dead". Spring was, however, under the impression that this measure would now be put on a statuary basis and was further angered when Reynolds in a Dáil answer to Fine Gael leader, John Bruton, said that he had no intention of legislating for it.

At this time Des O'Malley stepped down as leader of the P.D.s and was replaced by Mary Harney. O'Malley then announced that he would be running for Europe in the Munster Constituency which would be in direct competition to Pat Cox, the P.D. MEP. As a result Cox decided to run as an independent, a seat which he retained ironically at the expense of O'Malley. Though Fianna Fáil did extremely well in the European elections getting eight out of the fifteen seats, by losing a Bye-election to Democratic Left candidate, Erick Byrne in Dublin, and fine Gael's Michael Ring defeating Beverly Cooper-Flynn in Mayo, Fianna Fáil were now put in a position that a 'Rainbow Coalition' made up of Fine Gael, Labour and the P.D.s could oust Fianna Fáil. Though Spring realised this, Reynolds ignored it as he felt Labour would not chance an election due to their poor showing in the European elections, together with Spring's bad judgement of backing Orla Guerin as the Labour Candidate for Dublin in Europe and she been beaten by Labour's Bernie Malone.

The next major issue that could have a bearing on the sensitive situation of the Fianna Fáil/Labour coalition was, of course, the Beef Tribunal. Here Spring and Reynolds had an agreement that whatever the result and recommendation of the Tribunal, would be implemented. The Terms of Reference of the Tribunal had been widened to cover the whole beef industry from the original Goodman /Haughey relationship. This had been brought about by pressure from Spring and Des O'Malley. Then, as Justice Hamilton was about to report, there was an insinuation from Fine Gael's Jim Mitchell that Justice Hamilton may not be fully impartial as he may not want to implicate Ministers in the present Government who could have a say in Hamilton's promotion from his position of President of the High Court to Chief Justice. Mitchell's remarks caused consternation in the Dáil and next day he was forced to admit that he was not questioning Justice Hamilton's integrity. Then, Emily O'Reilly ran a story in the *Sunday Business Post* with the headline – "Spring Ready to Leave Coalition if Tribunal Report Censures Reynolds", of which Reynolds blamed Fergus Finlay and said, "no Government could survive this kind of thing".

The report of the Tribunal finally saw the light of day on the last Friday of July, the Bank Holiday weekend when it was delivered to the

Department of Agriculture. From there it was quickly despatched to the Taoiseach's Department. There, the nine hundred page report was divided up between the Taoiseach's team of Henry Hickey, Connor Maguire, Paddy Teahon, Frank Murray, Tom Savage, Donal Cronin and Seán Duignan. Each person, having read their piece, came to the conclusion that Reynolds had been vindicated and his integrity not questioned. This having been re-affirmed, Reynolds wanted the press immediately informed that his good name had been vindicated. Duignan and others advised Reynolds that this was not a good idea as there was an agreement with the Labour party that the report should be studied by Government before a statement be made. Reynolds, however, insisted that Duignan should meet the political correspondents immediately, but he first got permission to talk to his equivalent in the Labour party, John Kelly. Kelly was totally against going to the press but Duignan continued to prepare his statement for the press. Fergus Finlay flew back from holidays and was advised by Spring to go with Niall Burgess to Government Buildings and pick up their copy and to then join up with Greg Sparks and Willie Scally to study it. When they got to the offices of the Taoiseach, they found that they were locked and they could get no answer. They then went to Duignan's office where the phone was ringing, and Finlay picked up the phone to be told by RTÉ's Donal Kelly that he was expecting a statement. In walked Duignan, w ho took the phone from Finlay and told Kelly he would ring him back. A row ensued between Duignan and Finlay, with the non-elected Finlay's parting shot that "this could be the end of the Government. You have been warned". Later, in a conversation with Finlay, Spring stated, "Collective responsibility my eye. How can I stay in Government when I can't speak to my Taoiseach?" Later still Spring eventually got through and talked to Reynolds. Angry exchanges took place. Then Reynolds said to Spring, "You would not deny me my day in the sun", to which Spring replied, "There might not be any sun". Though they patched up their immediate differences and the Government survived, it was plain that it was only a matter of time before it would all end. At this time also, Bruton offered Spring a way out into a 'Rainbow Coalition', which was now possible due to the numbers game as a result of Fianna Fáil losses in bye-elections.

Spring Pulls the Rug on Coalition

Throughout the summer of 1994 Reynolds was getting impatient with the doddering of Sinn Féin on a response to the Joint Declaration of December 1993 and he was also fed up with the delaying tactics of the IRA with regards to a ceasefire. Although by now very few believed that a ceasefire would occur, Reynolds, due to information he had from senior republicans, was optimistic. In August, a US delegation led by Bill Flynn and including Niall O'Dowd and Bruce Morrison dropped into Reynolds on their way north to meet Gerry Adams. They were taken aback when in response to their suggestion of a temporary ceasefire Reynolds said that he was demanding a permanent ceasefire and he wanted it written in simple language that a child could understand. He added that when people enter the political arena there should be no need for guns. He was holding out for nothing else. Unbelievably, with a few little favours like getting President Clinton to organise a visa for Joe Cahill to go to the US to pull in the republicans there to agree to a ceasefire, he got his way. The IRA announced their ceasefire on 31st August, 1994. The questions that arose then as to whether it was a permanent ceasefire or not, can not take away from the fact that it was a moment of historic significance. In ten years it has only been broken once, with the massive explosion of Canary Wharf in London in early 1995. This happened while the Fine Gael/Labour coalition was in government and would probably have not occurred if the Reynolds' government was still in power.

The issue that was to spell the end of the Fianna Fáil/Labour Coalition was the connection between the case of paedophile priest Brendan Smith and the Attorney General's Office. The Attorney General at the time of the case was Harry Whelehan and he was the person chosen for President of the High Court by Albert Reynolds, against the wishes of Dick Spring – an issue that itself had nearly toppled the sensitive Government just weeks previously.

When Reynolds had proposed Whelehan for the job, Spring objected on the basis that he was too conservative and he wanted a more liberal agenda in that position. Reynolds stated that being conservative should not preclude a person from the position, that he felt he was the best person for the job and it was the custom over the years to give the job to the Attorney General. The news of this disagreement was spun to the media by Labour, while the Taoiseach was on an enterprise mission to Hong Kong, Australia and New Zealand. Spring said that the Labour party were proposing Justice Susan Denham for the position, even though she declared that she was not interested and had not been asked by the Labour Party if she was interested. A telephone conversation between the Taoiseach and the Tánaiste did not settle the disagreement. When the Taoiseach returned to Ireland on October 11th he arranged to meet Spring at Baldonnel Airport. Having come through Shannon where there was an aborted meeting with Boris Yeltsin, Premier of Russia, who was too sick/drunk to get off the plane, he eventually met Spring at midnight at Baldonnel, stating that they must both be mad to be having surreptitious meetings at outlandish times to discuss Government business. Spring also needed some time to sell the agreement.

A few days before the Baldonnel meeting a programme on UTV about a paedophile priest, Brendan Smith, was to have major repercussions for Reynolds, Whelehan and indeed the Government itself. On Thursday, October 11th Reynolds, Spring and Whelehan had a pre-Cabinet meeting to discuss Whelehan report on how he, as Attorney General, had handled the Brendan Smith case. After the meeting Spring was not happy with the report and let Reynolds know in writing of same. Next morning Labour deputies were given a copy of Whelehan's report. In the report Whelehan stood by the way his office handled the Smith case, that the case was the first time that the 1987 Extradition Act had been used in an extradition case and that it had involved unprecedented issues of law. At four o'clock that afternoon, as the nomination of Whelehan was being proposed, Spring led his Labour Ministers on a walk-out of the Cabinet meeting. The remaining Fianna Fáil Ministers proceeded with the nomination of Whelehan as President of the High Court and at half past five went to President at Áras an Uachtarán where Whelehan was appointed by President Robinson to that position and Eoin Fitzsimons was appointed to the position of Attorney General. On Sunday the Labour parliamentary party met for seven hours. Spring said he felt that the coalition was being abandoned by Fianna Fáil. At the end of the meeting he got permission from his colleagues to continue or pull out of the coalition as he wished. On Monday a copy of the report from Harry Whelehan appeared in the daily newspapers. The new Attorney General, Eoin Fitzsimons, having now studied the case, informed Reynolds that this was not the first case for extradition to be taken under the 1987 Extradition Act as had been stated by the previous Attorney General, Whelehan, in his report. A previous case of alleged sexual offences by an ex-monk, John Duggan, had been speedily processed in Whelehan's office in 1992 and that Duggan had been extradited and sentenced.

The next day John Bruton, leader of Fine Gael, puts down a motion of no confidence in the Government. Harry Whelehan was sworn in at a ceremony in the Supreme Court and his successor as Attorney General, Fitzsimons, was introduced to the Dáil. In the Dáil, Taoiseach Reynolds stated that the Smith case in no way impinged on the integrity of Whelehan as Attorney General or his new position as President of the High Court. Labour did not think Reynolds' speech was an adequate explanation. Next morning Fianna Fáil Ministers informed their Labour colleagues that as a result of 'new information coming to light', Whelehan's report was misleading. Spring then signs an agreement with Reynolds to stay in the Coalition and complete their 'Programme for Government'. Later in the day Spring meets Attorney General Eoin Fitzsimons from whom he finds out in the course of the conversation that he had informed Reynolds of the Duggan case on Monday, the day before Reynolds had exonerated Whelehan from blame in the Dáil. Spring meets Reynolds at noon and tells him the deal is off. To now save the Government, Justice Minister Máire Geoghan-Quinn offers her resignation to Reynolds, which he refuses to accept. Later that evening Reynolds tells the Dáil that after his statement to the Dáil on Tuesday he had received a letter from the new Attorney General, Fitzsimons, pointing out the importance of the Duggan case, that he now accepted Spring's reservations of Whelehan and that he regretted that he had appointed him as President of the High Court. This was not enough however, and Spring informed the Dáil that he and his colleagues were resigning from the Dáil even before the vote of no confidence. At ten thirty next morning, Albert Reynolds announced his resignation to the Dáil and stated he would not be seeking a dissolution of the Dáil. At one o'clock he tendered his resignation to President Robinson and at four o'clock Harry Whelehan resigned. It was a sad day in the history of Fianna Fáil and indeed a sad end to Albert Reynolds as Taoiseach. It practically put an end to a political career of a man, who in two short years as Taoiseach, had made a major contribution in his Peace process, oversaw an economy that was on the way up, unemployment on the way down and the country heading for the Celtic Tiger era. One could say that the directness and stubbornness that made him a millionaire, a politician, a Minister and a Taoiseach, who brought about the Downing Street Declaration and an IRA ceasefire was the characteristic that was his downfall in dealing with the rather vacillating Labour Party. The funny thing about it all is that the ordinary Labour T.D.s and even the Labour Ministers did not think that the Harry Whelehan dilemma was an election issue. It was the leaders' struggle and Spring being influenced by the non-elected trio of Finlay, Scalley and Sparks that eventually was to bring the fall of a successful Coalition but also the demise of the Labour Party and the end of Spring's leadership.

When Reynolds stepped down as Taoiseach, he also relinquished leadership of the Fianna Fáil. The ironic thing was that Harry Whelehan should resign from the Presidency of the High Court only hours later. If he had done so twenty-four hours earlier he could have saved Reynolds and the Government. On hearing of Whelehan's resignation, certain pro-

Reynolds supporters wanted to reverse the decision as Fianna Fáil leader, but the pro-Haughey faction, which included Burke, Ahern and P.J. Mara, ensured that this would not happen. As it happened, Ahern became leader of the party without a vote as Máire Geoghan-Quinn, the other candidate, realised that she did not have numbers and pulled out before a vote was necessary. Thus Ahern, at forty-three, became the youngest ever leader of the Fianna Fáil party.

After he became leader he held a meeting of the parliamentary party in the Burlington Hotel and talked of his intention to unify the party after twenty years of internal disquiet. He also put his cards on the table about his private life, his separation from his wife and his second relationship with Celia Larkin. Now that Reynolds was gone and Ahern was leader, it seemed a foregone conclusion that Fianna Fáil and Labour would now pick up the pieces and continue the Programme for Government which, apart form the personalities, was a successful partnership. Meetings began with Máire Geoghan-Quinn and Michael Smith representing Fianna Fáil and Pat Magnier and Brendan Howlin for Labour. When the Fianna Fáil delegates informed the Labour representatives that if they did not want Ray Burke in the Cabinet that would be all right. Since Labour had not requested this and although rumours abounded about Burke at the time, it caused the Labour representatives to wonder why Fianna Fáil had vouched this information. Spring did not read into it too much as he felt he could not interfere in choosing the Fianna Fáil team. However, a number of other things occurred that began casting doubt in the mind of Labour. John Bruton, in a newspaper article, accused Spring of planning to go back into Government with a party that caused the fall of the Government. But the straw that broke the camel's back was an article by Geraldine Kennedy that reminded everyone that the Fianna Fáil Ministers, including Ahern, had known the significance of the Duggan case Monday, November 14th. Ahern asked Fitzsimons to come up with a report as to how the Coalition collapsed. On this day Ahern was in Brussels and Reynolds in Copenhagen. A copy of the report was faxed to Reynolds in Budapest and he insisted on Spring not getting a copy till he had read it completely, although Spring was screaming for a copy. This did not help the relationship, and although Ahern gave a copy to Spring that night, it was too late and at two o'clock on Tuesday, 6th December, Spring dropped a bombshell by ringing Bertie and telling him the deal was off and he was banished to leader of the opposition for the next two years.

Ahern the Reuniter of the Party

Bertie Ahern was born in the Rotunda Hospital, on 12th September 1951. His father Con, a Corkonian who went to live in Dublin, had republican links going back to the time he was a member of the IRA under the command of Tom Barry and remained a strong republican. His name was on the record of 'the usual suspects' until the Gardaí, having raided his house after the murder of Garda Frank Fallon in April 1970, reckoned he was too old to be involved and took his name off that list. His mother Julia also came from a strong Cork republican family. Bertie had two brothers and two sisters. His brothers, Noel and Maurice, were also to follow Bertie into Dáil Éireann. Bertie's father was manager of the All Hallows farm, so though living in the city, Bertie had knowledge of farming and horticulture as he helped his father with the milking and feeding from a very young age. In addition, he spent his holidays from school working on the farm and became familiar with growing cauliflowers, celery and cabbages. If that was not enough, his holidays with his cousins in Cork would give him further knowledge of the farming way of life. Locally he would be in touch with the activities of the city and would have known the ins and outs of local politics by listening to local heavyweights, Noel Booth and Tom Houlihan, who were constant visitors to his parents' home.

His first real introduction to active politics was when asked by his teacher, Stan O'Brien, a Fianna Fáil candidate in a bye-election, to put up posters in the constituency. Together with his schoolmates they did a wonderful job of not alone erecting the posters, but ensuring they stayed up. Though O'Brien was not successful, Bertie not alone got the title of 'King of the Posterboys', but also got a good glimpse of what was to be one day his own constituency.

His education route started in St. Patrick's Primary School in Drumcondra and from there to St. Aidan's Secondary School where he passed his Leaving Certificate. He then attended the College of Commerce in Rathmines where he took his accountancy qualification and finished off by taking a diploma in tax, business administration and computer studies at the London School of Economics. His pre-political career was made up of a brief term with Bord Bainne followed by the job of assistant accountant at the Mater Hospital. Along with religion and politics, sport, particularly GAA, the main topics of conversation in the Ahern household in his home, it is no wonder that the young Ahern developed a passion for sport, which is still one of the pleasures of the simple life he leads outside his political life today. Though he did not break any records as a sportsman, he played in the Co. Dublin GAA competitions with Whitehall Colmcille's. He also played soccer for Home Farm and Drumcondra and helped to set up and play for St. Haller's Soccer club which then and now play in the Dublin Amateur League. His keen interest today is shown by his visits to Lansdowne Road, Old Trafford and Celtic Park to see the Irish, Manchester United and Celtic soccer teams in action as well as rarely missing a day at Croke Park when the 'Dubs' are in action.

His real political journey started with his involvement with the O'Donovan Rossa cumman where he became secretary, and with the help of John Booth, got involved with the organising committee there, and then on to be a member of the constituency organising committee. At this stage he backed the long-serving deputy Celia Lynch, while he invoked the help of a small clique of Tom Kitt, Senator Daithi O'Bhroinn and Paul Kiely, who became the team which helped him on his path to the Dáil. From 1969 onwards he also had a very close connection with the Trade Union movement where he had a part-time position as scrutineer and came into contact with such union activists and Jim Larkin Jnr., Paddy Cardiff and John Foster. These contacts became very useful later on when he was Minister for Labour putting the Social Partnership together. His contacts on the ground floor within the union was often better than some union officials themselves and it is well known that when the Financial Services Centre was being built, an electrician's dispute was settled by a visit by Labour Minister Ahern himself to his local trade union contacts without ever referring to the union officials.

In 1977 Bertie and a group of Fianna Fáil activists put together a study that predicted that a 5% swing for the party in Dublin would give Fianna Fáil an overall majority. This was given to Seamus Brennan, the then General Secretary of the party, who showed a keen interest in the study, which was also featured in Brian Farrell's RTÉ programme *7 Days*. As this was election year the Minister for Local Government in the Fine Gael/Labour Coalition Government, Jim Tully, did a major reconstruction of the constituencies which became known as 'Tullymander'. This was an attempt to ensure that the Coalition would remain in power. As the media and the public were giving no hint of a change it looked safe enough for the Coalition partners. They had not however envisaged the Fianna Fáil Manifesto which abolished rates on houses and tax on cars, as well as a lot more 'goodies'. As far as Bertie Ahern was concerned, the Tullymander did him a favour. The three-seat constituency strategy of the Coalition pushed Drumcondra and Glasnevin into Fianna Fáil's Jim Tunney area. As Tunney's stronghold was Finglas, he felt that there should be a candidate in the Drumcondra/Glasnevin area to pick up votes there. Though Bertie was defeated by Danny Bell for the party nomination, he was later imposed by headquarters and proved their faith in him by picking up 4,000 votes and gaining the second seat for them in the constituency. Bertie had arrived in Dáil Éireann and his prediction that Fianna Fáil would get an overall majority was more than had been imagined – thanks to a Manifesto. However the Manifesto, which was put together by Trinity economist Martin O'Donoghue, and whose Keynesian programme was to pump prime the economy, later was to become a cropper as it was not suitable for an open economy. Its features on tax and rates however, appealed to the electorate and ensured that Fianna Fáil got back to power with a twenty seat majority, its biggest ever, and again ensured that a Fine Gael led Coalition would not achieve two consecutive terms.

Now, in a close-knit Cabinet dominated by a small clique of Lynch, Colley, O'Malley and O'Donoghue, which later was to be its downfall, Ahern was very much lost in the huge number of backbenchers. He did not waste his time though and concentrated in learning all about legislation in the Dáil Library, streamlining his constituency and later keeping an eye on the succession stakes, when the backbenchers revolted against Lynch's style of government. By this time also, Charlie Haughey had worked his way back from the Arms Trial and had been made Minister for Health and Social Welfare. As Ahern admits, he "had never put his foot inside the Taoiseach's office", and through his association with the Mater had worked with Charlie Haughey on a committee, set up by Haughey when he was Shadow Spokesman on Health, and whose positiveness he admired, it was obvious whose side he would take in the election for Leader of the party and Taoiseach. When Lynch stepped down suddenly and created the leadership contest Ahern nailed his colours to the mast and went for Haughey. As he said, "I don't buy my colours coming out of the stadium". In the first Haughey Government he was made Assistant Chief Whip – a rather minor position – but as luck would have it for Ahern, the Chief Whip, Seán Moore, was ill for the year and Ahern was in fact the Acting Chief Whip. In this position he was able to meet with all the Fianna Fáil deputies and their constituencies, whipping the T.D.s up for voting and negotiating with opposition T.D.s for the first time and getting him into a power base at an early part of his political career. To add to Ahern's luck, his fellow constituent deputy, Jim Tunney, was made a Junior Minister for Education, with responsibility for sport, and he resigned his seat on Dublin Corporation and handed it over to Ahern, who was now in City Hall and all the local power that that can ensure.

Ahern finally becomes Taoiseach

After the disappointment of the previous let-down by Dick Spring and Labour, Ahern, was at last what he had once written in an essay as a schoolboy – Taoiseach of his country. With the Coalition agreement with the P.D.s and the support of independents Jackie Healy-Rae, Mildred Fox and Harry Blaney, Ahern was voted in as Taoiseach and he now set about appointing a Cabinet, again bearing in mind the unification of the party. Charlie McCreevey was at last in a position that suited him best – Minister for Finance; John O'Donoghue was given Justice; Mary O'Rourke, Public Enterprise; Michael Martin, Education; Dermot Ahearn, Social Welfare; Brian Cowen, Health; Joe Walsh, Agriculture; and Noel Dempsey, Environment. David Andrews was appointed Minister for Defence and Junior Minister for Foreign Affairs but, on an objection from Bruton that you could not be a Minister in one department and a Junior Minister in another, Ahern withdrew the junior position from him. The Foreign Affairs portfolio was again a problem when it came to selecting the senior Minister. At a press conference during the election campaign Geraldine Kennedy, *The Irish Times*, asked Ahern about alleged planning irregularities against Ray Burke. Ahern, without mentioning Burke's name, though stating "we all know who we are talking about", said he had spoken to the member on four occasions and was satisfied with his reply. On that basis the story died. After the election Ahern decided that before he handed the Foreign Affairs Ministry to Burke he would carry out some more investigations into the allegations. He sent his Chief Whip, Dermot Ahern to London to meet Joe Murphy, Chief Executive of JMSE, and was told by Murphy that no money was paid to Burke for political or planning favours. Ahern himself had made inquiries with builder Michael Bailey, another name in the planning saga. Having assured himself, and having consulted with Mary Harney, PD leader, he went ahead and appointed Ray Burke to the position of Minister for Foreign Affairs.

Ahern, now in the driving seat, got into action on the North of Ireland question. After the failure of the previous coalition to maintain the ceasefire – it having ended in February 1996 – and their further failure to make any progress towards restoring the ceasefire, Ahern linked up immediately with the new UK premier, Tony Blair, and a new ceasefire was brokered in July 1997. The satisfaction with this achievement was short-lived however, as the Ray Burke saga raised its ugly head again, now, especially, as he was a senior minister. A leak of Dermot Ahern's London trip, the *Sunday Tribune's* mention of Burke's name and it being now admitted that £30,000 political contribution was paid to Burke, though any impropriety was denied, resurrected the whole thing again. Even though Ahern, on an RTE *This Week* interview, stated that he knew about the payment and was "up every tree in North Dublin" investigating it and was happy it was all proper, plus the fact that Mary Harney publicly defended Burke, the opposition refused to go away. The next dilemma for Ahern was the admission by Charlie Haughey at the McCracken Tribunal that he had misled the Tribunal and indeed his

The author pictured with An Taoiseach, Bertie Aherne.

own solicitors up to then, and that he knew in 1993 that his financial advisor, Des Traynor, had accepted £1.3 million on his behalf form Ben Dunne and that he had personally received £210,000 from Dunne. He stated that he had not been truthful as he was embarrassed at the public perception of him if these payments became public and was sorry he was not forthcoming from the start. He also stated that he had left all his personal financial affairs in the hands of his "trusted friend and financial advisor", Des Traynor, and now admitted that he should have "involved himself to a greater degree" in this regard.

The Burke saga however, would not go away and pressure from the media, the opposition and colleagues within his own party eventually led him to resigning from his ministry, his Dáil seat and creating a bye-election. It later transpired that Burke had also received another £30,000 from Rennicks, a Tony O'Reilly associate company. He eventually served a prison sentence for tax evasion and faces a €10 million legal bill as the state refuses to pick up his Tribunal costs as he had obstructed the Tribunal. As if that was not enough, a Roscommon builder in the UK, Tom Gilmartin, initiated allegations against the late Liam Lawlor, former Fianna Fáil TD for West County Dublin, and former Fianna Fáil Minister and European Commissioner Padraig Flynn of accepting monies form him with regard to various planning applications in Dublin. Other embarrassments were that Lawlor was a member of the Dáil Ethics Committee at the time of the alleged payments, and as well as that, Padraic Flynn's daughter, Beverley Cooper Flynn, had allegations against her by a Meath farmer of offering him tax evading advice when selling insurance policies for the National Irish Bank. To add to Ahern's misery in such a short time span when it was found that Michael Collins, T.D. for West Limerick to have not paid taxes on all his income though he had made a declaration of tax compliance after the May 2002 General Election. There was still more, as North Kerry T.D., Denis Foley, who was a member of the Public Accounts Committee, was found also to have had a bogus offshore account.

The author with Dick Roche, Minister for the Environment.

Cooper-Flynn, Foley, Collins and Lawlor were all expelled form the party, though Ahern still had to depend on their votes to keep the party in power.

Attempts have been made from time to time to link Ahern with some or all of these wrongdoings but nobody has ever been able to come up with one shred of evidence to that effect.

The author with Mary Coughlan, Minister for Agriculture and Food.

Ahern's Second Term as Taoiseach

At the beginning of 2003 Ahern and Fianna Fáil were to start experiencing major problems. As the opposition was rather weak, Fianna Fáil can only blame themselves for the dilemma. February saw a dip in an MRSI poll for both the Taoiseach and the Government. This was followed at the end of March by a similar poll by the IMS/Irish Independent poll. Some of the reasons for the setback were that it was perceived that the Government were not delivering on election promises, which were being brought about by a downturn in the economy

Bertie Ahern in Washington.

which looked like the end of the Celtic Tiger. Cutbacks in health and education seemed to be the main culprits and these were being highlighted in the media, especially the radio, either by concerned people or opposition politicking. All these were having negative effects on the Government. This often led to nasty behaviour like booing the Taoiseach at the opening of the Special Olympics and at a football match at Croke Parke. There was also criticism of the fact that the Taoiseach's daughter decided to have her wedding in France and be covered by the *Hello* magazine. It was not at all a nice year for Bertie Ahern as he also experienced the end of a fifteen-year relationship with Celia Larkin, a major personal trauma for anybody on its own. It was also a year that the Government brought in the ending of the dual mandate, where from now on, T.D.s and Senators could no longer hold onto their Council seats as well. This rancoured with even members of the Fianna Fáil party, as an attempt to do it the previous year had been blocked by independents who were holding the balance of power. Things in the North were not going anywhere as the Government and the UK were waiting for an IRA commitment that the war in the North was over. Other areas of note were the disputes over the ban on the building of one-off housing in the countryside, which seemed to be 'the urban side telling the rural side what to do', and the whole policy seeming to contradict the Spatial Strategy and Decentralisation. The Taoiseach counteracted this by releasing more state lands for housing at affordable prices. Ahern also came in for some criticism from Ryanair chief, Michael O'Leary, about the lack of decision making on the opening up of Dublin Airport to private competition and break the monopoly of Aer Rianta. Other issues concerned the benchmarking process for public service pay. Towards the end of the year it could be shown however, that things that had been put in place by the Government were turning the economy around again. Inflation had been brought down to 2.3% (EU 2%+), Unemployment 4.3% (EU 8.8%) and Growth 2% (EU 0.3%).

2004 was a very significant year for Ahern as he started the year as President of the European Union, testified before the Mahon Tribunal, presided over the enlargement of the EU (bringing in ten more East European states) and carried out a reshuffle of the Cabinet. September saw the party holding a major conference in Inchidoney addressed by socialist priest Fr. Seán Healy, to re-emphasise the party as a party with a socialist focus and not being pulled to the right by the Progressive Democrats. They felt that they were been seen to be too dominated by the pro-business, tax-cutting, privatisation-minded P.D.s, as the opposition and the media were insisting. Bertie, as President of the European Council, brought the twin problems of the EU Constitution and finding a candidate to be the President of the European Parliament to a successful conclusion. For a while it was thought that he, himself, would fit the bill as EU President, but he quickly reiterated his commitment to national politics. Internationally he also played host to US President George W. Bush. Here he played another stormer as he not only alone reassured the continuing friendship between Ireland and the United States, but was also able to put across our joint battle against world terror and Ireland's and Europe's legitimate concerns, particularly regarding the treatment of prisoners in Iraq and Guantanamo Bay. However, his successes abroad did not seem to please the electorate as Fianna Fáil took a hammering in the European and Local Elections. A fiasco with and failure to bring in electronic voting which cost €50 million added to the woes of the government and gave a stick to wallop them with as the opposition rowed in with blaming the government for wasting money in one area and not spending it in other, needy areas such as Heath and Education. The reshuffle of the Cabinet was not as much as people expected. Brian Cowen replaced Charlie McCreevey in Finance and McCreevey was shipped off to Europe as Commissioner. In some areas, even within the party, it was thought that McCreevey was removed from finance as he was too right-wing and not in keeping with the Fianna Fáil 'socialist', caring image that the party was now trying to portray. There had been rumblings within the party by some T.D.s to get rid of McCreevey. The whole parliamentary party retreated in September to a major conference in Inchadoney in Cork to review their direction. Key speaker was well-knows socialist priest, Fr. Seán Healy, who had been an outspoken critic of Government policy with regards poverty in Ireland.

During these years the Tribunals were occasionally raising their ugly heads to create the odd headline in the media. Towards the end of 2004, a major bank robbery in the Northern Bank, being attributed to the IRA and the murder of Robert McCartney were not alone a setback for Sinn Féin, but also created further delays in the Northern Peace Process. However, a good budget in December which followed the 'Socialist' trend of the Inchidoney conference and gave the people some of the goodies promised at election time put the Government, and particularly back up in the February 2005 IMS/Irish Independent polls. Fianna Fáil were 42%, about the same percentage they were in the May 2002 General Election. This was a big change from the 30% which they obtained in the EU and Local elections of June 2004. The latest opinion poll also put a Fianna Fáil/P.D. Government at 49% as against a Fine Gael/Labour coalition at 38%. An MRBI poll on Sinn Féin in March said they were unlikely to return to violence (44%), were responsible for the Northern Bank robbery (64%) and would be unacceptable to be part of a coalition (56%). In January, the Taoiseach showed that he was keeping his eye on the international trade opportunities for Ireland as he took the largest trade delegation ever from Ireland to China, which is experiencing one of the fastest growth rates in the world. The delegation, which included the Taoiseach himself, Enterprise Minister Michael Martin, Minister for Agriculture, Mary Coughlan and Minister for Education, Mary Hannifin. Between them they tied up agreements for over €170 million, which could reach €4 billion in the next three to five years. In education alone, there is huge scope for increase as we only account for 3,000 of the 500,000 Chinese third level students that go abroad every year for their education. With regards to Agriculture, our beef is barred from the Chinese markets due to the fear of BSE, whereas Minister Martin, having signed agreements for €39 million, saw further openings between Irish and Chinese companies for software, telecommunications and medical products. By June there seemed to be attempts by both Fianna Fáil and the P.D.s to start looking at the next election. The P.D.s may have got the Inchidoney message and were preparing and hinting at, at least, that they were open to other coalitions. The Café Bar Bill by Justice Minister Michael McDowell was shot down in Cabinet by Fianna Fáil, the seeming lack of cooperation in the Defamation Bill and the Anti-Social Bill and the reversal of the Nigerian Leaving Certificate student deportation by Brian Cowen seemed to cause strains in the Government partners and they set about separate identities for the 2007 General Election.

The criticism of the Gardaí Bill by the Morris Tribunal hasn't helped either. A poll in June saw Fianna Fáil down on previous polls by 6%. Together with the 4% for the P.D.s leave them trailing behind Fine Gael (25%) and Labour (14%). Apart from the above, Fianna Fáil/P.D. squabbles, there were certain other contributing factors to this result.

Firstly there was now the likelihood of a pre-election pact between Fine Gael and Labour. While the economy, per say, seemed to be on the up again, the constant focus by the opposition and the media on the Health Services seemed to be getting through to 'the dogs in the street', and Mary Harney, now in charge of Health, did not seem to be able to act fast enough to put out any fires. A court ruling that deductions taken from pensioners by State Institutions over the years were illegal added to the problems. An RTE *Prime Time* programme exposed the treatment of residents of a nursing home in Swords and this opened up a whole new can of worms of how the elderly were being treated by State-funded institutions. Shortly before the poll, Professor Brendan Drumm turned down the position of head of the Health Services Executive due to a dispute with Health Minister Harney. Professor Drumm later accepted the post. The government and Justice Minister McDowell were also coming in for criticism for their handing of the McBrearty case and the way the injustice was handled. One could say that a lot of the troubles that Fianna Fáil were experiencing were P.D. led. Two Bye-elections occurred in this period due to John Bruton standing down in Meath when he was appointed EU Ambassador to the US, and Charlie McCreevey in North Kildare being chosen as EU Commissioner. Major delays and bumbling by Fianna Fáil left them very late in selecting candidates. In Kildare, both Charlie McCreevey Junior and Paul Kelly, who went close to winning a seat in 2002 decided not to run, leaving them with a third choice candidate. The chosen candidate in Meath, Cllr. Tommy Reilly decided to step down after a media campaign that linked a land deal he had done with controversial lobbyist, Frank Dunlop, though no impropriety had been done. The results of the Bye-election were that Shane McEntee retained John Bruton's seat for Fine Gael and an Independent, Catherine Murphy took the North Kildare seat from Fianna Fáil.

In spite of the sniping from the Opposition, and tribunals which brought certain former members of the party into controversy, Fianna Fáil, under Ahern's leadership has experienced a continuation of the Celtic Tiger, giving Ireland one of the highest GNP growth rates in the world and making it the fourth richest country in world.

2006 began in a high for the Government and the Fianna Fáil party in general. In India a road called after the founder, Éamon de Valéra, was being opened in New Delhi and Taoiseach, Bertie Ahern took the oppertunity to take a trade Mission to that country, as he had done to China a year earlier. The group included enterprise Minister, Michael Martin, education Minister Mary Hannifin and Tourism Minister, John O'Donoghue, together with a host of companies, doing business or hoping to do business in a country with a population of 1.1 billion people and a GNP that is growing at 8% pa. This and the fact that India is the third largest economy in Asia after Japan and China. Of course 2006 is also the year that celebrates two major anniversaries;- The 90th anniversary of the Easter Rising and the 80th anniversary of the founding of the Fianna Fáil party. The Taoiseach launched the anniversary of the Rising at the Ard Fheis when he declared 'The Irish people need to reclaim the spirit of 1916, which is not the property of those, who have abused and debased the title of republicism'. The celebration itself on Easter Monday consisted of 2,500 soldiers marching up O'Connell St., a display of military equipment, a fly-over by the Air Corp, and a showing of the Navy. An army officer read the proclamation of independence at the G.P.O. The aftermath of the Celebrations was to increase Fianna Fáil's rating by 5 points in a Sunday Business/Red C poll to 28%, which was one of Fianna Fáil's highest ratings in a number of years ,though it still fell short of the 42% in 2002 and pre-1997 election rating when it was in the mid-40s. The 80th anniversary celebrations of Fianna Fáil, which brings me to the end of this history, was another whopping success for the party and the speech given by the Taoiseach is an indication of the party's commitment to the future. Mr. Ahearn recalled Fianna Fáil's historical foundations, a foundation in which a clear vision will be built. The programme will encompass the 'best traditions' of Fianna Fáil and will embrace social responsibility and community.' Fianna Fáil is committed to using this nation's hard earned and long awaited economic stability to put in place a credible republican programme. In our view the only republican programme is one with a sound fiscal policy'. The programme will tackle social injustice and continue to prioritise the delivery of well paid jobs. It will focus on childhood poverty, educational disadvantage and care for senior citizens. 'In short it is a programme which implicitly respects both the traditions of this party and the dignity and will of the Irish people. This is the programme that Fianna Fáil will continue to implement in Government'. He spoke of the need to develop a new sense of community spirit among all our citizens living in Ireland. "Our true richness as a people depends on the quality of life in Irish society. For all the welcome of economic and political progress, Fianna Fáil is determined that we do not lose of the challenge to embrace a renewed sense of spirit in our communities. In our time, by fostering strong communities, which will thrive due to the willingness of our people to become active and participate, we too want to reinvigorate a strong sense of citizenship and give the people a greater sense of ownership in both their own localities and the life of the country. The programme will also consider the changing nature of Irish society, a society now enriched by an international mix of culture and tradition. We believe that it is our responsibility now to ensure, every single person on this island, irrespective of class, colour or creed is given the opportunity to live the dream of freedom and prosperity, which the generations before us at home and abroad sacrificed so much to make possible. Peace, justice, unity and prosperity must always be the aims we seek to fulfil in a spirit of social partnership, community, solidarity and national freedom".